How to Scrapbook

Joy Aitman & Sarah McKenna

SEARCH PRESS

First published in 2005 by

Search Press Limited
Wellwood, North Farm Road,
Tunbridge Wells, Kent TN2 3DR

Reprinted 2006, 2007 (twice)

Based on the following books from the Scrapbooking series
published by Search Press:

Start Scrapbooking by Joy Aitman (2005)
Eyelets for Scrapbooks by Sarah McKenna (2005)
Cropping for Scrapbooks by Sarah McKenna (2005)

Text copyright © Joy Aitman, Sarah McKenna

Photographs by Charlotte de la Bédoyère, Search Press Studios
and by Roddy Paine Photographic Studios
Photographs and design copyright © Search Press Ltd 2006
First published in hardback by Search Press Ltd 2005

PB:
ISBN 10: 1 84448 154 9 / IBSN 13: 978 184448 154 5

HB:
ISBN 10: 1 84448 122 0 / ISBN 13: 978 184448 122 4

Suppliers
If you have difficulty in obtaining any of the materials and
equipment mentioned in this book, then please write to the
Publishers, at the address above, for a current list of stockists,
including firms who operate a mail-order service. This list also
details some of the fonts used in scrapbooking projects.

How to Scrapbook

Joy Aitman & Sarah McKenna

Venice

Norfolk
Squashy
Lara
Fay
(visiting dogs)!

Mystery Play
Fundraising

La Pigeonnier
Najac

North Yorkshire

MOET   MOET

Contents

*Dedicated to the
memory of my Mum,
Evelyn Scott, who gave
me so many precious
moments to scrapbook.*

Monica & Joseph

September 12ᵗʰ

1959

Salisbury

Rhodesia

Start Scrapbooking

Joy Aitman

Introduction

My love of scrapbooking began five years ago. I have always been a keen photographer and dabbled in many crafts. Scrapbooking was the missing link: it brought the crafts and the photography together.

With four children, I take lots of photographs. I have recorded all the important events in their lives and of course all those little moments that do not seem so important at the time. They each have a scrapbook album which chronicles their life so far and they get lots of enjoyment from reading it themselves and showing it off to others.

Scrapbooking is also a fantastic way to keep a diary of the year. We scrapbook birthday parties, holidays, days out, school events and seasonal celebrations. I always try to have my camera with me, although photographs are not always necessary to create a layout.

The pages can be as simple or as complicated as you want them to be. It is a hobby you can do on your own or you can join others for a crop to swap ideas and show off layouts. It is also a hobby which spans the generations. Grandparents, parents and children can sit down together and create a scrapbook to pass on for the enjoyment of future generations.

I hope that you enjoy the projects in this section and that you will be searching out your old photographs and mementoes to create a scrapbook of your own. This section gives you the basic techniques and some ideas to get you started. As soon as you start sorting through your own photographs, you will be brimming over with ideas for your own layouts. Happy sorting and happy scrapping.

Materials

The materials for scrapbooking must be of a quality that will preserve your photographs and memorabilia. Materials used in the past such as sugar paper books, sticky tape, gum type glue and 'magnetic' albums with sticky strips were damaging to photographs.

Albums, card, paper, pens and adhesives must be acid free. Acid in paper or card causes the paper itself to deteriorate and also migrates into photographs, turning them yellow, faded and brittle. Acidic adhesives can literally eat away the emulsion from photographs. Paper should also be lignin free, since lignin causes the paper to brown and crumble.

Buy scrapbooking products from well-known scrapbooking companies and learn to look at labels. You should be looking for acid free, photo-safe or archival quality.

Granny and baby
In the bottom right-hand corner you can see where the acid adhesive has eaten away the emulsion from the photograph.

Two girls
This is a colour photograph from the 1970s that has changed colour because it was kept in an unsuitable album.

Nurses
Here the photographic emulsion has been eaten away at the edges and from behind, causing extensive damage to the image.

Basic equipment

You do not need too many pieces of equipment to scrapbook but there are some essentials.

A personal trimmer or **mini guillotine** makes cropping your photographs quicker and easier, eliminating wobbly edges caused by scissors. They are safe for children to use.

Scissors should be comfortable and suitable for the task. I use a small, sharp pair for cutting around lettering or small shapes, and a larger pair for general cutting.

It is important to choose the right **adhesive** for the job. Double-sided **photo stickers** or **tape**, which comes on a runner, are suitable for photographs. So is **repositionable tape**, which is useful for attaching items temporarily and becomes permanent if left. Never use a wet adhesive for photographs. **Glue dots** are essential for sticking down heavy embellishments. A **glue pen** is handy for small paper items such as punched shapes. **PVA glue** is a good, strong adhesive, useful for sticking down heavy embellishments.

Pens, used for journaling or decorating pages, should be acid free, waterproof and fade resistant. I have used calligraphy, fine point, double-ended and dotting pens.

Clockwise from bottom left: dotting, calligraphy, fine point and double-ended pens; a guillotine; paper scissors in two sizes; PVA glue with an applicator; an acid-free glue pen; a roll of glue dots, a repositionable tape runner and photo stickers.

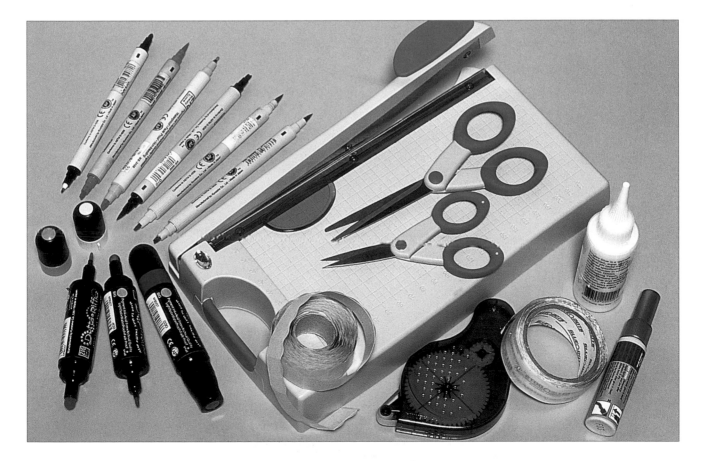

Albums

Albums should be acid free and sturdy. They come in a number of different styles and sizes but there are three basic types.

Ring-bound albums are very basic. They contain top-loading page protectors, which you fill with your finished layouts. They cannot be extended in any way.

Strap-bound albums are pages connected with flexible plastic straps. You work directly on to the pages and then cover them with slip-over protectors. They can be extended by threading more pages on to the strap.

Post-bound albums contain page protectors bound together with two to three screw posts. You put your finished layouts into the protectors back to back. They can be extended by using extension posts. They make it easiest to rearrange the order of your layouts and are my favourite.

The most popular size of album is 30.5 x 30.5cm (12 x 12in). Most cardstock and paper is cut to that size. Smaller albums are available in 21.6 x 28cm (8½ x 11in), 20.3 x 20.3cm (8 x 8in) and 15.2 x 15.2 (6 x 6in). These make good gift albums.

A selection of albums in different styles and sizes.

Paper

Cardstock is the mainstay of your album. It is cut in sizes to fit your album but usually comes in 30.5 x 30.5cm (12 x 12in). This is what you use as the background for your layouts, the mats for your photographs and for making embellishments. Make sure it is not too thick (160g is best). It must be acid and lignin free as it will be in direct contact with your photographs. A good scrapbooker will have a variety of colours on hand.

A good selection of **printed paper** will complement your cardstock. This is very much up to personal choice but do not let the patterns detract from your photographs. If the budget allows a few **specialist papers**, handmade, silk papers or vellums are always an attractive addition to a page.

Cardstock made to fit albums shown with a selection of papers and vellums used to decorate scrapbook pages.

Embellishments

I love bumpy pages and use a variety of embellishments on my layouts. However, do try and choose flattish objects to avoid tearing page protectors or damaging photographs on other layouts.

Wire is great for creating your own embellishments. It comes in a variety of different colours and thicknesses and can be easily shaped. It should be cut using **wire cutters**, not your scissors. I like to use it with **buttons** in all different themes or **beads**, especially seed beads and alphabet beads.

Paper punches provide a variety of shapes for your layouts. Punch out paper, card, cork and metal.

Fibres can be used to loop through tags or form borders. You can also thread a **needle** and stitch with fibres. They come in luscious colours and textures.

Tags can be all different shapes and types, from luggage tags to metal-rimmed circles. Use pre-made tags or create your own.

Fabric and **haberdashery** such as ribbons, twill tape and embroidery silks are becoming increasingly popular.

A **paper piercer** and **cork mat** will help you create holes for sewing.

Metal embellishments can give your pages a more masculine look. I love charms, washers and hinges**.**

Self-adhesive mesh comes in a variety of colours and can make great borders.

Coloured glue sticks and a **hot glue gun** can be used to create faux wax seals. Rub them with **gilt wax** to make them extra special.

Gesso creates a surface on embellishments which will hold chalks and paints.

Jigsaw pieces can be coloured with chalks to match your layout.

Paper punches, twill tape, fibres, a paper piercer and cork mat, needles, wire cutters, eyelets and snaps, beads and alphabet beads, charms and washers, wire, tags and envelopes, self-adhesive mesh, glue sticks with a hot glue gun and tile, white gesso, gilt paste and jigsaw pieces.

Other materials

A **30.5cm (12in) paper trimmer** is useful for cutting large pieces of cardstock. Every scrapbooker has a favourite. They come with a variety of cutting methods: sliding, rotary or guillotine blades.

A **craft knife** has a number of uses. I particularly like them for cutting out titles. It is good to try a few different ones to find one that is comfortable for you. Make sure it has a safety cover. You will need to use it with a **cutting mat.** Choose a mat with a grid on it as this will make cutting and measuring easier.

Rubber stamps can add decoration to a page, and letter stamps can be used for titles or journaling. The **inkpads** must contain permanent and acid free ink.

A **heating tool** can be applied to stamped images and embossing powder to create some interesting effects.

Decorating chalks can be used to add colour. They can also be used to age pieces of card or embellishments.

An **eyelet tool kit** is used to attach eyelets and snaps, which are eyelets without the central hole on the front. They both make wonderful embellishments as well as fixing other elements in place. The kit consists of a hammer, setting mat, hole punch with a variety of different sized holes, and a setter to open out the backs of the eyelets or snaps and hold them firm.

A heating tool, paper trimmer, alphabet rubber stamps, eyelet tool kit, craft knives, blades and cutting mat, rubber stamps, decorating chalks and inkpad.

Techniques

Cropping

Cropping is the term used for cutting your photographs. This is done if you are not happy with their composition or content. We do not always take perfect photographs, and cropping will remove the empty spaces, the people we did not want, or those stray items that creep in at the edges. However, it is important that you do not remove all the background from photographs, as you want to be able to set the scene and tell a story. Never cut polaroids as you will release chemicals which will leak out and spoil your pages. Heritage photographs should be treated with great respect as you are unlikely to have the negatives. Keep them whole to preserve historical detail. You can colour copy heritage photographs if there is something you would like to crop.

Look carefully at your photographs. Choose five to six for your layout. Determine what you will need to crop to focus on the theme of your layout. You can leave some photographs whole – do not get too carried away!

If you want to give cropped photographs a straight edge, use your mini guillotine to crop them. You can also use a template and scissors or a cutting system to cut them into other shapes such as circles or ovals.

Paula's wedding day
Wedding photographs look particularly good cropped into ovals.

Duncan goes exploring
This picture remains uncropped to emphasise the smallness and the adventurous nature of the boy.

A very windswept Rosie
Crop away all the background to make the subject fill the frame.

Not many of us can take the perfect photograph. By cropping them we can make them look better. We can remove excess background, unwanted people or objects, blurs or flashbacks.

These photographs are shown uncropped on the right, and cropped below.

Duncan rolls away

The excess space has been removed from the top and side of this photograph.

Washing Dad's car

The top has been taken off to remove the car from the girl's head. A small section has then been removed from the side to balance the shape of the photograph.

Helping Daddy

A section has been taken from the right-hand side to remove the toppled chair.

17

Matting

Matting is the process of putting photographs on a coloured cardstock mat. This can add definition to your photograph, enhance the colours and add interest to the page. Photographs can be matted in a number of different ways, but the simplest way is shown below.

1. Apply glue to the back of your photograph using repositionable tape as shown here. You can also use photo stickers.

2. Leave a small border. To help you to get the photograph straight, try to line up its edges with the machine-cut edges of the cardstock.

3. Cut round the image using scissors and leaving a border of backing card.

4. Use the guillotine to trim one side of the cardstock to match the borders on the other sides. Trim the remaining side to match and you are ready to position the matted photograph on your layout.

On the boardwalk

A photograph mat does not need to be a solid piece of card.

Grace

A torn mat can be very effective.

Kate and Wayne's wedding

A simple, classic mat is the most suitable for wedding photographs.

St. Ives

Have fun experimenting with different types of matting.

Choosing colour

Choosing the colours on your page is a very personal thing. We all have our favourite colour palettes; however, choosing the right colours is the key to a good page. Colour creates the mood and can enhance the photographs. New scrapbookers often find it difficult to choose and worry that they will make the wrong choice. Remember that the colours must ultimately please you and will reflect your personality. A colour wheel can be a useful addition to your tool bag as an aid to choosing combinations of colours.

When creating a layout there are two simple ways to choose your colours: firstly, being led by the colours in the photograph. By looking at the photographs you can often select colours that match or complement those that you can see. Do not choose more than four colours as this will confuse the eye. In the example I have selected two; the red from the jacket and the blue from the trim. I will use the tartan from the skirt as an embellishment.

Colour choice led by the photograph

Here the photograph itself has led the choice of cardstock colour and embellishments.

Blue for a boy

Traditional blue was chosen to complement the black and white baby photograph below, whereas Christmas themed colours work well in the page on the left.

Secondly by considering the theme of the layout; people tend to associate particular colours with events, celebrations, moods or seasons. A Christmas layout (below) could have red, green and gold; beach layouts blue and sand; baby layouts blue or pink. In the example shown right the photograph is black and white so I had no colour reference points. The baby is a boy, so I have chosen a very traditional blue for my cardstock, patterned paper and embellishments.

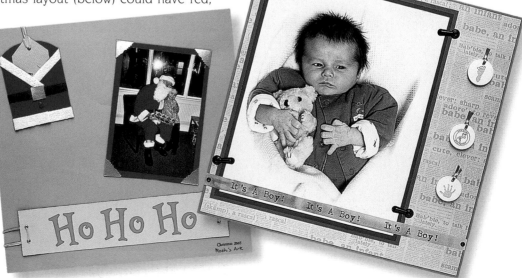

It is best to start with two colours, one for your background and one for your mat. Other colours can be added with embellishments. Lay the photograph on both colours and decide which way round looks best. A very light or dark photograph can be transformed by the colour you choose to mat it on. A dark photograph can be lifted with a light mat and a light photograph can be muted on a dark mat. The coloured mat will also define the edges of the photograph and make them stand out on the page. For some special photographs you may want to double or triple mat them.

Bounce

In this layout I have looked at the colours in the t-shirt and have been led by them. I matted the photograph on the lighter blue because the colours in the background of the photograph are quite dark. Although there is a lot of green in the photograph I felt that if I selected green cardstock as well, the whole layout would become dominated by green.

Layout

The first thing you need to decide is whether you are creating a single or double-page layout. This will influence how many photographs you use and how you arrange them. There is no correct number of photographs to put on a layout. It is not unusual to create a layout with a single photograph or capture an event with ten to twelve photographs. Be led by how many photographs you have taken – you may need to create an entire album for a special event! Choose a theme for your page; this will help you choose colours and embellishments.

Apart from your photographs, you will also need to think about the placement of a title, journaling and embellishments and arranging them to create a balanced layout.

There is usually a logical order to a series of photographs from an event. They make most sense if they are arranged chronologically. There may be one photograph that is a key focus, and that should be given predominance.

Sometimes a layout comes together very quickly, other times you feel as if you are solving a jigsaw puzzle. It is worth persevering to get it right, but remember, every layout does not have to be perfect.

Discover

This double-page layout has eight photographs on it but it does not look crowded. There is plenty of space separating each element. The shape and positioning of the photographs makes the two pages mirror images of each other, and this helps to balance the layout.

Brother and sister

This is a single-page layout and you can clearly see where I have divided the page vertically into thirds. The various elements are then positioned within their own third to create a balanced page.

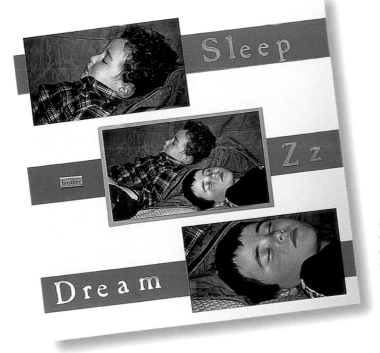

Sleep

This is a single-page layout with three quite large photographs. I have created balance by dividing the page into thirds in both directions and placing the page elements at key points within this grid.

Journaling

Journaling is the documenting of facts or feelings on the page. It helps you to remember and to tell the story to others looking at your album whether in the past or the present. You can write as little or as much as you want to, but do write something. It is a good prompt to use the four Ws: who, what, when and where? This is useful historical documentation for future generations. You may also want to include quotations, poems or song lyrics.

There are different ways to journal and it is nice to incorporate a variety of methods in your album.

Handwriting

By writing on your page I feel that you leave a little bit of yourself on the layout, stamping your personality and style for others to enjoy. It does not matter if you do not like your own handwriting, nobody ever does!

Choose your pens from the wide selection that is available, making sure they are acid free. Fine liners, calligraphy pens and dot pens can be used on their own or together.

Practise what you are going to write so that you know how much space you will need. Use pencil lines as a guide, and erase them later.

Embellishing your title with flowers

1. You can create flowers to decorate handwriting. Make a dot on scrap paper with a dark marker pen. Press the pink pen to the blender pen.

2. Touch the the dark dot with the blender pen.

3. Do your handwriting in pencil. Press the blender pen down on the writing to make flower shapes.

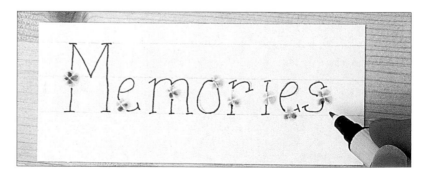

4. Go over the pencilled writing with a black pen.

Layered writing

Build up layers with different shades of the same colour. Start with the lightest first. Experiment with different pens to achieve different effects. Scroll and brush pens are a lot of fun.

1. You can layer writing with brush pens. Write in pencil first, then go over it with the first colour.

2. Then go over it with a second pen in a different tone of the same colour.

Shadowed writing

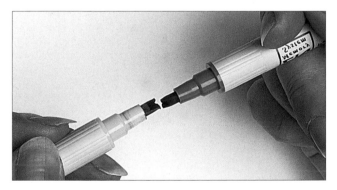

1. For another effect, press the scroll end of a pen against another colour.

2. Write with the first pen to create a shadowed effect.

Dot writing

Simple writing can be made more interesting with the addition of dots.

Using envelopes, pockets and mini-books

These are a different way to journal, so that your journaling does not have to be on display if you want to keep it personal. They are fun to create and they can be quite decorative. You can use pre-made items or make your own to match your layout.

1. More personal things can be written in a concertina style 'book'.

2. This is then tied up with a ribbon.

Time layout

Write on tags placed in simple stitched pockets.

Baby layout

A letter can be tucked into a small vellum envelope.

Using alphabet stamps

Alphabet stamps are available in a number of different styles and sizes. Look for ones that suit your style of scrapbooking. Experiment with the effects that you can achieve by stamping on to different surfaces. Chalks can be used to create a more subtle, pastel effect. Stamp using a watermark pad and then dust with the chalks using a cotton wool ball. By combining different colours of chalk you can achieve very different looks.

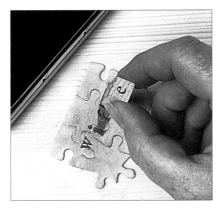

1. Take some pieces from a cheap cardboard jigsaw. Paint over the pictures using white acrylic gesso or paint.

2. When the paint is dry, use a make-up applicator to apply coloured chalk.

3. Use a black inkpad and alphabet stamps to stamp the words you need on to the jigsaw pieces.

Pieces of me

Create your own embellishments and personalise them using alphabet stamps.

Printing

Journaling can be printed on to a variety of surfaces including tags, vellums, acetates (ink-jet), twill tape, ribbon and fabric.

1. Print out your text on standard A4 printer paper.

2. Apply repositionable adhesive tape to the back of the item you wish to print on.

3. Fix it over the text, making sure it is secure.

4. Run the paper back through the printer, overprinting on to the item. Then you can peel off the item and rub off the adhesive.

Tip

If you are printing on acetate or vellum, set your printer to the transparency setting.

January layout

Print on an ink-jet transparency to create a layered look. Experiment with different colours and fonts.

Daffodils layout

Print on to vellum and lay it over a photograph for a soft look.

Using alphabet beads, buttons and charms

This is a fun way of creating titles or highlighting particular words in your journaling. The beads and buttons can be stuck down individually or threaded on to wire to create words. The metal charms can be stuck or eyeleted on. Try different combinations of styles, colours and materials.

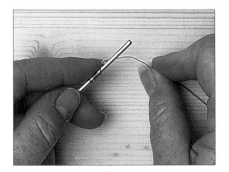

1. Take a length of 24 gauge wire and wind it round a small post to create a spiral at one end.

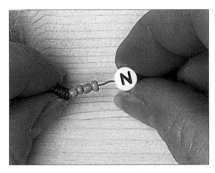

2. Thread your beads and alphabet beads on to the straight section of the wire.

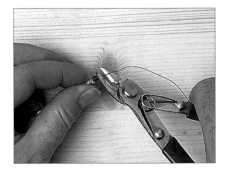

3. When you have finished threading on the beads, make another spiral at the end and trim the wire using wire cutters.

4. Press a glue dot on to the back of each alphabet bead and attach the beaded wire to your design.

A simple tag embellishment for a Christmas layout using seed and alphabet beads.

Duncan

A title can be created using a combination of glass and alphabet beads.

Using eyelets

Eyelets can be functional or decorative on a page. They are metal, usually aluminium, and will not rust. They come in a variety of shapes, sizes and colours, but they are all set in the same way.

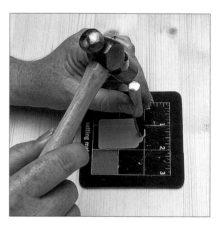

1. Mark on your card where you wish to make the hole for your eyelet. Select the size of the hole to match your eyelet. Place your card on a setting mat. Do not use your cutting mat as it will be damaged. Hold the punch upright with your fingers close to the paper. Strike the punch firmly with the hammer. You should be able to punch through one layer of card with one hit.

2. Put the neck of the eyelet through the hole.

3. Turn over the card so that the neck of the eyelet is facing up. Place the right sized setter head into the neck of the eyelet. Strike firmly with the hammer. The back of the eyelet will now flatten to look like a flower.

4. Remove the setter and hammer the eyelet once more to make sure it is flush to the paper.

The finished tag. Placing an eyelet in the hole makes it look more professional.

Using eyelets to attach four corners

When you attach a piece of card, paper or vellum by four corners it is important that you follow the correct order to prevent twisting.

1. Place a small strip of repositionable adhesive on the reverse of the item you want to eyelet. Mark where you are going to make the holes.

2. Place on to the layout and punch the first hole in the top left-hand corner. Set the eyelet. Punch the hole in the top right-hand corner and set the eyelet. If you are using vellum, remove the repositionable adhesive. You can now punch and set the other two holes.

Using eyelets for decoration

Eyelets can be used on their own to create simple embellishments or combined with other elements.

Embellishments

Embellishments can make your page look extra special. They can be as simple or as complicated as you wish. Do take care not to over-embellish your page: remember your photographs are the most important element on the page.

Wire, button and bead border

Wire is one of my favourite embellishments. It is very versatile and easy to use. It can be curled, twisted and shaped. It can be used for threading buttons and beads on and it comes in a variety of colours and thicknesses. The higher the gauge, the finer the wire.

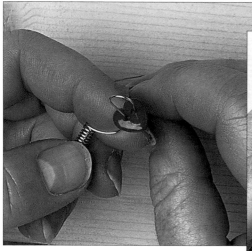

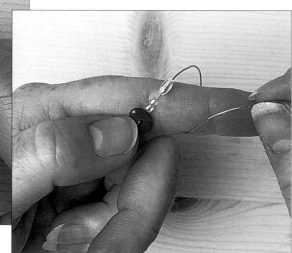

1. Cut the wire double the length of the border. Thread the wire through the holes on the first button as if you are making a stitch. Pull tight to secure the button. Leave a 6cm (2⅜in) tail.

2. Make a loop in the wire and thread on some beads and the second button. Repeat until your border is long enough. Leave a 6cm (2⅜in) tail.

The finished border. I have curled the tails at both ends round a skewer to create a spring shape. I have then stuck the border on to the cardstock by attaching glue dots to the buttons.

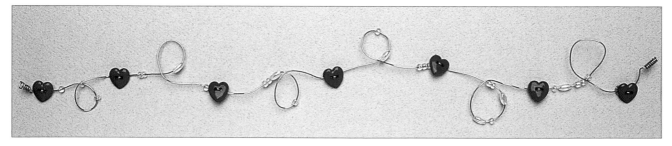

Using buttons with shanks

1. Cut the shank off the button with a pair of wire cutters. Cut as close to the base of the button as possible.

2. Stick the button on with a glue dot. This means you will not have to wait for the glue to dry.

Sunflower

Three sunflower buttons add colour to the layout.

Fibres and threads – stitching on the page

The secret to stitching on your page is to make the holes first using a template. This is particularly important if you are stitching a word.

1. Print out your word in the correct size and font. Attach to your layout with repositionable adhesive. Place the card on a mat – an old mouse mat would do, or a cork tile. Pierce holes with a paper piercer.

2. Remove the template and stitch with stranded embroidery thread in back stitch. Take care not to pull too tightly to avoid tearing the card.

The finished tag. I have added a 'sewn-on' patch and a ribbon in the same colour as the stitching.

Seaside Pictures

Most people have seaside pictures in their collections and like to scrapbook them to remember their holidays. These are always a good set of photographs to get you started in scrapbooking as they have a very definite theme. This makes choosing colours, patterned papers and embellishments much easier. My photographs are of an exotic trip to Indonesia.

You will need

Three photographs

30.5 x 30.5cm (12 x12in) cardstock: one sheet Pool blue; two sheets Cocoa brown

30.5 x 30.5cm (12 x12in) patterned paper: Antique maps

Repositionable tape

Gilt wax

Luggage tag

Blue hot glue stick

Mini hot glue gun

Blue fibres

Craft glue dots

Ceramic tile

Shell rubber stamp

Craft knife and cutting mat

Scissors

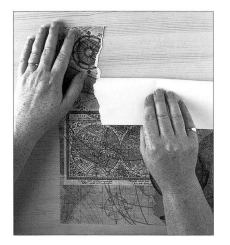

1. Tear the antique map paper to create a 7–8cm (2¾–3¼in) wide strip. Tear the paper towards you to expose the white layer.

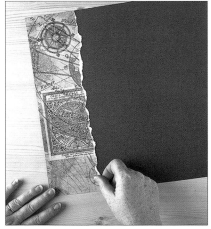

2. Use repositionable tape to stick the torn strip to the left-hand side of the brown card.

3. Place the photograph on the blue card and use scissors to cut round it, leaving an even border as shown.

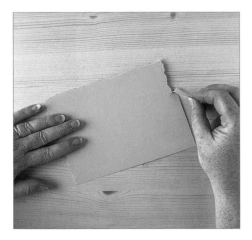

4. Tear the edges of the blue backing rectangle towards you.

5. Mat all the photographs in the same way and place two on the backing sheet of the left-hand page using repositionable tape.

6. Tear antique map paper to trim the right-hand side of the right-hand page and place the third photograph as shown.

7. Heat the hot glue gun with the blue glue stick inside. Squeeze a circle of glue approximately 3cm (1¼in) in diameter on to your tile.

8. Press the rubber stamp in to the glue and leave it to set. Remove the stamp.

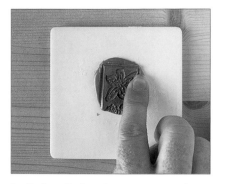  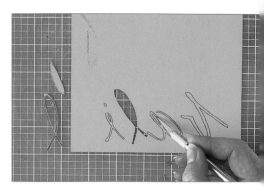

9. Rub a little gilt wax on to the 'seal' with your fingertip. A little goes a long way.

10. Print the luggage label with the place name and date, using the method shown on page 28.

11. Select an italic font and outline style and type your title. Use the draw program to flip the image vertically so that it is reversed, and print it on to blue cardstock. Cut it out with a craft knife or small scissors. The black outline will not show as it will be on the reverse.

Seaside Pictures

I particularly liked the antique map paper which gave the look of a more exotic destination. I chose a dark brown background to complement the turquoise blue of the sea and the sky in the photographs.

12. Assemble the two scrapbook pages and stick down the various elements. Use glue dots to attach the wax seal, glue pen for the cut-out lettering and repositionable tape for the luggage label.

St. Ives

Cornwall

February 2004

Duncan had a lovely time
playing on the beach. He
was happy to sit on his
own building castles.

[ad·ven´·ture]

sun   sea   sand

The beach in winter

*The colours and embellishments chosen reflect the cold and ruggedness of a
winter beach.*

sand

sticks

castle

success (lŭk'sĕs') 1. a
favorable result 2. gaining
of wealth, fame or recognition
3. attaining one's aspirations.

Happy

Lazy days

St. Ives 2004

Sunset on the shore

The warmth of the sunset is captured with the use of brightly coloured transparencies and metallic slide mounts.

School Picture

We all have pictures of either ourselves as children, our own children or our grandchildren posing for their yearly school portrait photograph. It is a challenge to create a different layout for each photograph. In this layout I have attempted the look of a cork notice board decorated with a collection of school essentials.

You will need

School photograph

One 30.5 x 30.5cm (12 x 12in) piece of thin cork

Two pieces of 30.5 x 30.5cm (12 x 12in) red cardstock (or a colour to complement the school uniform)

Small brown envelope

10cm (4in) of white twill tape

Library card and envelope

Four 2mm (1/16in) mini snaps in primary colours

Scrap of note paper

A4 printer paper

Headed school notepaper

30.5cm (12in) paper trimmer or mini guillotine

Glue dots

Alphabet stamps

Black inkpad

Repositionable tape or photo stickers

Acid free pen

Eyelet tool kit

1. Use a paper trimmer or mini guillotine to trim the cork, taking 6mm (¼in) from the top and one side.

3. Use alphabet stamps and an inkpad to stamp the small brown envelope with the words 'lunch money'.

2. Use glue dots to attach the cork centrally on the backing card. Mat the photograph on card of the same colour, leaving a 5mm (³/₁₆ in) border all the way round, and place the matted photograph as shown on the cork 'notice board'.

4. Print out the child's name on an ordinary sheet of A4 paper. Position the length of twill tape over the lettering and print the name on the tape as shown on page 28.

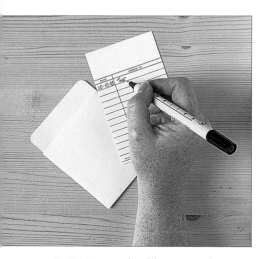

5. Write on the library card as shown.

6. Fix the snaps to each end of the name tag, following the same method as for eyelets shown on page 30.

7. Write on the scrap of notepaper and attach a snap to one corner. Tear off the corner of a letter from school which shows the school badge. Assemble the page as shown and stick everything down using repositionable tape or photo stickers.

Jake's year at school

This layout can be added to throughout the year, with tickets for the nativity play, a school council badge, or any other reminders – just like your notice board at home.

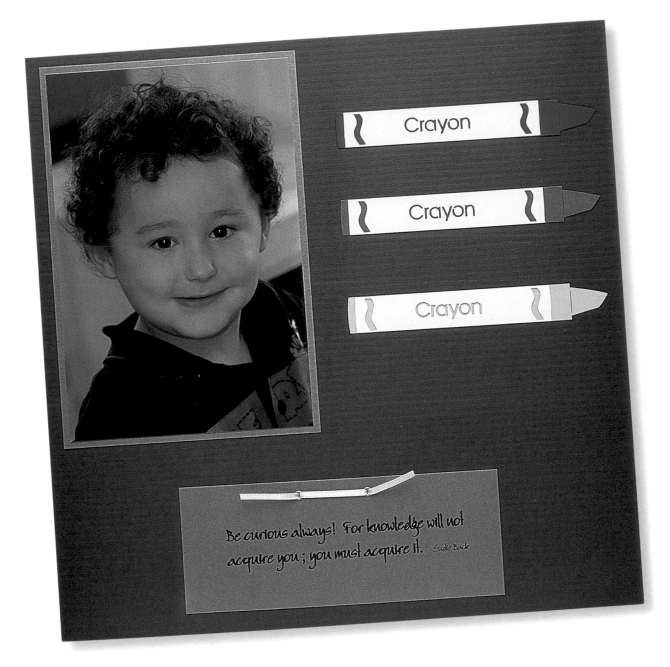

Be curious always! For knowledge will not acquire you; you must acquire it. *Sudie Back*

Nursery days

Children start school younger and younger. Don't forget to scrapbook nursery days as well.
Use an inspirational quotation for your title.

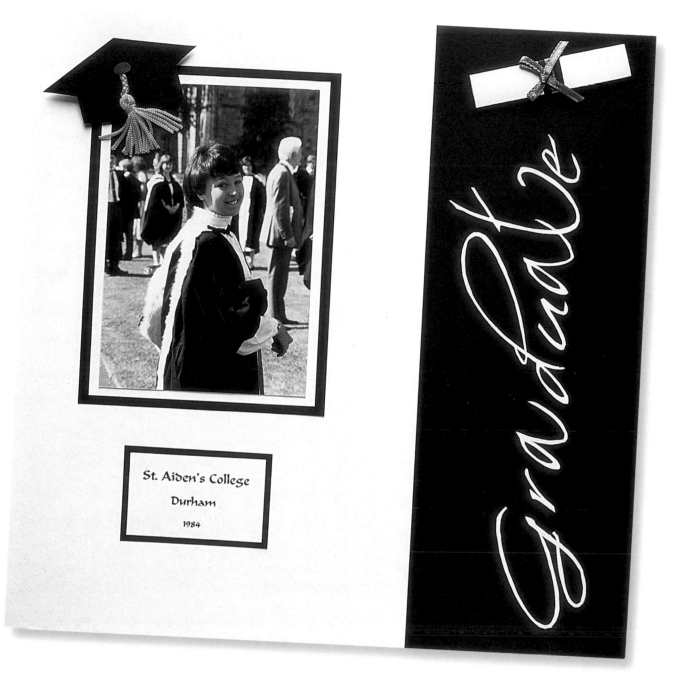

St. Aiden's College

Durham

1984

Graduation

A simple graduation layout using pre-made embellishments and a hand-cut title as
described on page 36.

Wedding Picture

We all take photographs, or have our photograph taken, at weddings. It is a special day and we want our layouts to look special too. I always think that wedding pages should be simple and clean cut so that the main focal point is the photograph.

Choose colours that match the wedding dress or the bridesmaids' dresses and if you are doing a whole album, repeat these on each page to tie all the pages together. Remember to include invitations, order of service sheets, menus, confetti and other mementoes of the day.

You will need

Wedding photograph

20.3 x 20.3cm (8 x 8in) ivory cardstock

20.3 x 20.3cm (8 x 8in) deep red cardstock for matting and embellishments

Scraps of dark green cardstock to make leaves

Pale green twill tape,
1.2 x 20.3cm (½ x 8in)

Three pewter 3mm (⅛in) eyelets

Repositionable tape or photo stickers

Glue dots

Double-sided tape

Eyelet tool kit

Mini guillotine

Scissors

1. Tear out three 40mm (1½in) diameter circles, three 35mm (1⅜in) diameter circles and three 30mm (1¼in) diameter circles in red card. Tear three leaf shapes approximately 30mm long from green card.

2. Crumple up all of your circles and leaves and then flatten them out. This gives the flowers a more three-dimensional look. Moisten your thumb and forefinger and use them to roll up the edges of the flowers, again to add dimension.

3. Layer the three sizes of circles to form three flowers and use the eyelet tool kit to secure a pewter eyelet in the centre of each one as shown on page 30.

4. Print your chosen quotation on twill tape as described on page 28. Mat the photograph and fix it on the page with repositionable tape or photo stickers. Attach the twill tape using double-sided tape.

5. Use glue dots to attach the flowers and leaves.

Grow old with me ... the best is yet to come

Red roses were the predominant theme of this page and the rest of the album.

Monica & Joseph

September 12th

1959

Salisbury

Rhodesia

Monica and Joseph

Older style or heritage wedding photographs look best with more subtle colours and appropriate embellishments such as ribbons and charms.

Dedication

For Emma, Annie, Charlsie and Katie, my very own
supermodels – with thanks!

Cropping for Scrapbooks

Sarah McKenna

Introduction

I have had a passion for photography ever since I was given a Box Brownie camera at the age of nine, but it was not until 1997 that a friend working in the States introduced me to scrapbooking. As soon as I realised the opportunities that scrapbooking provided for displaying photographs in an interesting and inventive way, as well as capturing the stories behind the pictures in writing, I was hooked!

Cropping is one of the basics of scrapbooking and I use it to enhance the photographs in my albums, either by cutting the photographs themselves or the card and paper around them. In this section, I will show you many different cropping techniques and suggest when they can be used to best effect. You will also discover how to add titles and journaling and how to create a variety of effects that add interest, definition and texture to your pages.

One of the great joys of scrapbooking is that there is no right or wrong way of doing it. I hope I can inspire you to experiment because scrapbooking is a very personal way of storing your memories. Try combining cropping techniques with other craft tools that you might already use such as punches, stickers, stamps and more. Above all, I hope you will be able to use the ideas in this section to create beautiful scrapbook pages that reflect you.

discover

LETTERS

KATIE

18 May 1998

Memories are the flowers in the garden of life......

TAKE TIME EVERY DAY TO BE SILLY!

Materials

There are only a few basic materials needed for scrapbooking: an album, cardstock to fit your album (the standard size is 30.5 x 30.5cm (12 x 12in) square), adhesive to fix the photographs and a pen or computer for adding text (this is known as journaling). Although these are the essentials, there are many additional materials that you can use on your album pages. Pages can be as simple or as complicated as you like and the crossover with other crafts, such as card making, sewing, collage, painting and rubber stamping, is enormous. It is essential that the paper, card and adhesive that touch your photographs are acid free so that your photographs are not damaged. Paper should also be lignin free otherwise it will deteriorate. I recommend that you buy material from reliable scrapbooking sources and look for labels which indicate that they are archival quality, photo-safe or acid free.

A guillotine and a smaller paper trimmer

Basic equipment

A **guillotine** capable of cutting 30.5 x 30.5cm (12 x 12in) cardstock is the best way to cut card and paper neatly and quickly. A **trimmer** or small guillotine is useful for smaller pieces of card and for photographs. **Scissors** are essential. I use a very small sharp pair for close cropping work, such as silhouetting.
Fancy-edged scissors are also available.
A **cutting mat** is necessary for use with a craft knife and other cutting tools. My cutting mat is self-healing and 33cm (13in) square which means I can work on a whole scrapbook page at once. It also has measurements marked on it, which is very useful. **Circle** and **oval cutters** come in a variety of designs which all work slightly differently. A **craft knife** allows you to cut accurately, for example, for hand-cut titles or where precise measurements are important, as with mosaics. I always use a cork-backed **metal ruler** as it works well with craft knives and does not slip. Unlike its acrylic counterpart, you cannot slice bits off it! **Craft punches** are used for punching out a variety of individual shapes from photographs, card or paper.
A **corner rounder** shapes the corners of card and photographs.

Clockwise from bottom right: fancy-edged scissors, small scissors, a craft knife, a corner rounder, craft punches in various sizes and designs, circle cutters, a cork-backed metal ruler and a self-healing cutting mat.

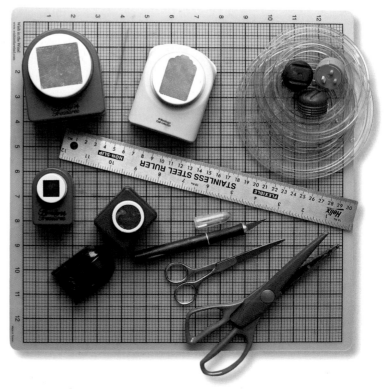

A **soft pencil, sharpener** and **eraser** will prove useful. A **photo-safe wax crayon** is helpful for marking cutting lines on photographs as it will not damage them and can be rubbed out later using a **photo-safe cloth**. Remove finger marks with **photograph cleaner**. **Gel pens** and **marker pens** are ideal for journaling and titles as long as they are acid free, fade resistant and waterproof. You can also create neat journaling with a more 'published' effect on a **computer**. Font packages are available on CD-ROM.

Adhesives come in many guises and you will probably need a variety of them for different purposes. **Photo tabs** and **double-sided tape** are useful for adhering cardstock, paper and photographs. **Glue pens** and **water-based adhesive** will fix light embellishments in place. Use **glue-dots** for attaching heavier bits and pieces. A regular **glue stick** is good for making items from cardstock, such as covering frames. **Repositionable tape** (available in a runner) is invaluable for temporarily attaching items while you consider your design. Finally, **adhesive remover** can be extremely useful if you need to take any part of your page apart!

Clockwise from bottom right: a soft pencil, photo-safe wax crayon, gel pens, marker pens, glue pen, water-based adhesive with nozzle, glue stick, repositionable tape in a tape runner, cleaning pad for use with photograph cleaner, photo-safe cloth, compact disc, large reel of double-sided tape, small reel of repositionable tape, box of photo tabs, glue dots in two different sizes, adhesive remover, photograph cleaner, eraser and pencil sharpener.

Paper and card

Most scrapbookers use standard cardstock squares to give a sturdy background to their layouts. Patterned or plain papers and various types of card are then added to create the page. Paper is available in a vast array of colours, textures and designs. What you choose will be determined by your own individual taste and the layout you are creating, but when you are selecting paper, ensure that it is acid and lignin free. Experiment with some of the lovely speciality papers available, such as vellum, textured paper or mesh, and use them to make interesting effects. However, your photographs are usually the focus of the page so keep to papers with subtle patterns and avoid designs that might be distracting, or use them sparingly. Acetate is useful for journaling and to create a layered look.

Cardstock, patterned paper, patterned vellum, plain paper, corrugated paper, embossed paper, plain vellum, mesh and acetate.

Albums

Albums come in a variety of sizes but the most popular in the UK is 30.5 x 30.5cm (12 x 12in). All of the layouts in this section were created on standard 30.5 x 30.5cm (12 x 12in) cardstock. Other sizes are available, for example 20.5 x 20.5cm (8 x 8in) and 15.5 x 15.5cm (6 x 6in), which make nice gift albums. Only use acid free albums. I find a top-loading album easiest to work with. The layouts are slipped into page protectors, which are then secured into the album on metal posts. This means that you can arrange the pages in any order, add extra pages if necessary and you do not have to work chronologically. Strap-bound albums, which have plastic straps to hook the pages on, are a popular alternative to top-loading albums.

A selection of 30.5 x 30.5cm (12 x 12in) and 20.5 x 20.5cm (8 x 8in) albums.

Embellishments

It is tempting to buy lots of the embellishments available but they are best used sparingly, otherwise they may overwhelm the page.

Raffia, leather thread and **ribbons** or any attractive fibres are all great for attaching and threading **charms, buttons** and **beads** as well as being attractive in their own right. Beads can also be stuck directly on to your card using **strong double-sided tape.** Explore the haberdashery section at your local craft shop: **decorative rick-rack** might be just what you are looking for! **Twill tape** is made of fabric so you can stamp and paint on to it, or even print on it using a computer. **Tags** come in a range of different guises, including **metal-rimmed tags**, or you can make your own. **Wire** comes in a range of gauges and can be used in a similar way to raffia and ribbon. It is best cut with **wire cutters** to save damaging your scissors. **Metal book frames** are popular embellishments, as are **hinges** and **washers**. Paper fasteners such as **brads** and **safety pins** add interesting detail and also have a practical use in fixing photographs and other elements to your page. **Craft stickers** are available in a huge range of designs and materials, including fabric and 3D plastic. Do not neglect your own tickets, tokens, cards, leaflets, maps and other **memorabilia** as these details make your pages truly personal. It is best to spray them with **archival mist** before adhering them to your pages to ensure archival quality is preserved. Unusual **postage stamps** and **cigarette cards** are worth considering. **Rub-on transfers** come as sheets of letters or words. You position them and then rub the front of the transfer evenly with a blunt pencil or lolly stick (see page 93).

Clockwise from top: sticky-back fabric stickers, brads, butterfly charm, safety pins, metal bookplates and fastenings, shells, buttons, reels of coloured wire, wire cutters, beads, strong double-sided tape, roll of raffia, fibres, leather, white twill tape, floral rick-rack, ribbons, stamps, sheet of letter stickers, tile-effect 3D craft stickers, patterned acetate, tags, metal-rimmed tags and cigarette cards.

Other materials

You can borrow the techniques and materials of almost any craft that you enjoy when scrapbooking.

I frequently use **acrylic paints** for areas of background because they give me the freedom to mix exactly the colours I want. You could also use watercolours. **Textured paste** gives a three-dimensional aspect to your work. This thick paste looks like toothpaste when you apply it but dries hard. Some varieties of textured paste contain sand or gems, but once it is completely dry, you can also paint directly on to it. I use **brushes** and **rollers** of various sizes with paints and textured paste to achieve different effects (see pages 92–93).

Eyelets are embellishments but they are also ideal for fastening vellum, acetate and any thin material where glue might show through. An **eyelet tool kit** consists of a hole punch, a hammer, a setter and a setting mat. After punching a hole through your cardstock, you set the eyelet in the hole.

To create a rustic or aged look, rub **pigment ink** in inkpads, **chalks** or **rub-on paints** along the straight or torn edges of cardstock and photographs. Coloured chalk can be applied with a **cotton wool make-up pad** or small **chalk applicator** (see page 79). Rub-on paints come in ready-made palettes and have the consistency of lipstick. You apply them, as the name suggests, by rubbing them on with your finger.

Rubber stamps are available in many designs and can be used to make wonderful effects with water-based paint, pigment ink or a **clear inkpad** and chalks. Applying more than one colour to a rubber stamp makes an interesting, mottled image (see the shell detail on page 83).

You can create stylish details with **embossing powder**, rubber stamps and a **heating tool**. The process is simple: press a rubber stamp into a clear inkpad, apply the stamp to your cardstock, shake embossing powder over the area and heat with the heating tool. The powder melts to give a raised, metallic finish in the shape of the rubber stamp (see page 79). I use **tweezers** to hold the card that I am embossing away from my fingers to avoid burning them!

There are many ways of creating lettering by hand (see pages 86–89), including using a **letter stencil** but you could invest in a **die cut machine** (right). A range of different fonts in many sizes and various dies are available for them.

Clockwise from top: a heating tool, clear inkpad, embossing powder, textured paste, plate, turquoise acrylic paint, white acrylic paint, paint brush, foam roller, sand, sandpaper, metallic rub-on paints, letter stencil, cotton wool make-up pad, chalks, small chalk applicator, eyelet tool kit and eyelets, tweezers, rubber stamps in different designs and pigment inkpads.

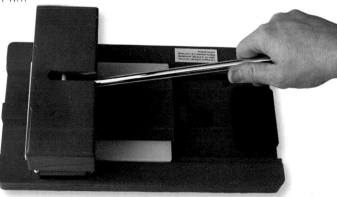

Basics

Photographs arranged on cardstock or paper and other card form the basis of an album page. Album pages are often referred to as 'layouts', particularly when the design spreads over two adjoining pages. Before you begin arranging photographs, card or paper on an album page, it is often necessary to cut the photographs to size in some way and this is known as 'cropping'.

Cropping has many advantages. You can focus attention on a certain part of the photograph by cutting out any distracting background. You can cut a photograph in any number of ways, and each one will create a completely different design. In a sense, it is 'photo art'. Sometimes, cropping simply allows you to fit more photographs on your page.

The market

I love the colour and vibrancy of the produce in foreign markets and wanted to create a layout that really emphasised this. The photographs for this page were cropped into 5 x 7.5cm (2 x 3in) rectangles using a trimmer.

Cutting

Craft knife

When you are using a craft knife, always cut on a cutting mat. To make straight, accurate lines, hold the edge of the blade against a cork-backed metal ruler. Press and angle the craft knife slightly towards the ruler when cutting.

Trimmer or guillotine

A trimmer is ideal for cutting small sections of photograph and card. Measurements marked on the trimmer make it easy to cut several pieces to the same size quickly. A larger guillotine is useful for cutting whole sheets of cardstock or larger photographs.

Scissors

A small pair of sharp scissors is invaluable for all close cropping work such as silhouetting (see page 84) and cutting out lettering (see page 86).

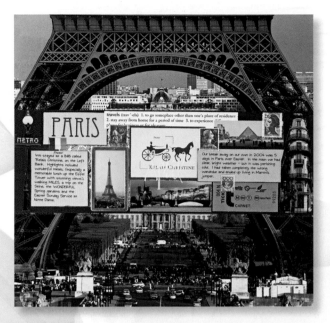

Paris

Here I have sliced a 30.5 x 20cm (12 x 8in) photograph in half, fixing each half to the top and bottom of the scrapbook page. I have then added a band of montage in the middle. The montage includes carefully cut photographs, journaling and memorabilia. This helps to give an impression of the holiday whilst stressing the monolithic structure that is the Eiffel Tower, which dominates the page just as it dominates the Paris skyline.

Circle cutters

You will be able to produce perfect circles if you invest in a set of circle cutters. These are cleverly designed so that you can combine the circles and blades in many different ways. For example, you can create a cardstock circle that is fractionally larger than your picture and this is ideal for creating a border (see 'Matting', page 60). Similar sets are also available in ovals.

1. Place the clear plastic circle over the relevant part of the photograph and position the cutting blade against it.

2. Drag the cutting blade all the way round the plastic circle. Then you can remove the cut-out circle.

Abigail and Sophie

Many of these photographs had distracting backgrounds. I cut them all into circles to focus attention on the children. Circles create a softer look than squares or rectangles. The montage in the middle follows the baby theme.

Matting

Matting your photographs is a basic scrapbooking technique. It involves sticking a photograph on to cardstock or paper and cutting round it to create a border. Matting enhances your photographs, adding interest and definition and creates a focal point on your page. There are various different methods of matting, depending upon the result you are trying to achieve. In this chapter I have explained some ideas that you will be able to adapt and use on your layouts.

1. Arrange three photographs on your backing card, allowing enough space between them to create a border. Keep any off-cuts of card for other projects.

2. When you are happy with the arrangement, remove one photograph at a time, attach photo tabs to the back and fix it in place on the backing card.

3. Line your card up on a guillotine so that the blade is parallel to the first photograph. Slice quickly and smoothly. When you reposition the mounted photograph to cut the next side, make sure that the space between the blade and the photograph is the same as it was before so that the border will be even. Repeat with your other photographs.

Tip
To get the cleanest cut from a guillotine, always pull the cutting blade slightly towards the guillotine itself as you cut downwards.

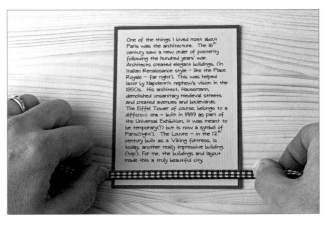

4. Double mount a fourth photograph using different coloured card. Now arrange all of your matted photographs on your page.

5. Write or type your chosen text neatly on to card and mat the card. Add a decorative detail such as ribbon. The ribbon pictured was fixed using repositionable tape.

Paris in the Springtime

The finished page. The mats around these pictures are quite narrow so that there is only a hint of colour. This looks more sophisticated than thick mats and keeps the focus on the photographs.

Matting a tag

Tags are available commercially but not necessarily in the size or colour that is right for your particular project. Making your own tag is the answer. This example uses a photograph but tags can feature journaling, stamping or any kind of embellishment.

1. To assess which area of the photograph you want to appear on your tag, hold it against a light with the back facing you. Roughly mark the edges of your tag shape using a photo-safe wax crayon.

2. Following your marks, cut away the long sides of the photograph. Draw a horizontal line 2.5cm (1in) down from the top and then two matching diagonal lines to create the tag shape.

3. Double mount the photograph and tear off, rather than cut, the bottom of the second piece of card.

4. Attach a sticker or a punched out shape to the top of the tag. Then, using an eyelet tool kit, hammer a hole through the sticker.

5. Thread attractive fibres through the hole.

Tip
Yellow is a very strong colour on layouts. I always work on the basis that a little bit of yellow goes a very long way!

Sharing a lilo!

Here is a photographic sequence of my daughter and me demonstrating how not to share a lilo! I have used turquoise and white to complement the pool water, with punched sun shapes providing splashes of yellow to give the impression of summer.

Matting a detail

This technique allows you to draw attention to a focal point in a photograph whilst preserving the background. I have used it here on an enlarged print but it works on smaller photographs, too.

1. Use repositionable tape to stick your photograph to the cutting mat. Draw a square around your chosen detail using a photo-safe wax crayon. Use a craft knife and metal ruler to cut it out.

2. Mat the cut-out detail and then position it back in its original place. Attach the matted detail using photo tabs.

Winter

Living in the middle of rural Gloucestershire can have its advantages. When it snows heavily, our lovely scenery changes into a winter wonderland. On the day pictured here, the roads and schools were closed so we set off to a friend's farm in the next valley to go sledging. For this layout, I wanted to highlight our little troop walking through the magical landscape. For me, the pictures say it all. A happy day indeed!

Composing a page

The very first thing I do before cutting any photographs or even choosing colours and card, is decide what type of page or layout I am trying to create. For example, am I trying to display a single photograph or perhaps a number of photographs of an occasion over a two-page layout? This will determine the size of the layout.

Mood

Next, I decide what mood I am trying to capture. So, my second question when planning a page or layout is, 'What is the main message I want to convey?' It might be happy, serious, fun, active or contemplative. The mood of the photograph should be your starting point and it will affect your choice of colours, textures and embellishments. I have created pages for four very different photographs to illustrate this point.

Tip

I rarely crop heritage photographs. Their original style usually adds to the aged theme.

Wedding

This black and white photograph has a nostalgic, romantic feel so I have chosen softly patterned papers and vellum, tearing the edges to make them softer still. Silver edging on the vellum and tag, foil embellishments and some silver embossing add to the sense of celebration. Gold would also work well with the wedding theme but I prefer silver with black and white photographs. Although you can put virtually any colour with black and white photographs, I have used a deep, cranberry-coloured background. For me, this helps to focus on the serious side of a wedding. Bright red or turquoise would have gone with the photograph but would not have conveyed the right mood at all.

Sassy

This photograph of my daughter Emma is really punchy; it jumps off the page. It was important not to drown it in detail but to keep the uncomplicated, striking look. I have chosen simple but vividly coloured lines and a hand-cut title in a contemporary font style. The colours, including the black background, add to the modern feel. The red picks up the red in the photograph and lime green adds just a touch of interest without being overwhelming. Note that the red photograph mat is very thin, which is part of the graphic style.

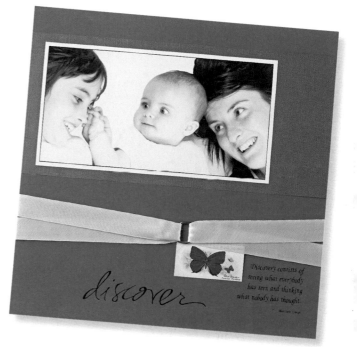

Family

This is a lovely, soft and feminine shot of mother, baby and older daughter. Traditionally, babies are associated with pastel colours but my personal preference is for colours with more depth. I have chosen relatively muted colours because I do not want to ruin the soft theme, but they are not as 'wishy-washy' as pastel shades. I want the photograph to be the focus so I have kept the embellishments very simple with the baby blue ribbon my sole concession to pastels!

Sisters

Although the pose in this photograph is quite static, the bright sunlight and Katie's jazzy top scream summer fun. When choosing paper for my pages, I often take photographs to the craft shop with me so that I can match colours and designs. I felt that I had to design the page around Katie's top and the photograph can take bright colours and boldly patterned paper. I was lucky, the paper manufacturer might almost have modelled the design of the paper on Katie's summer vest! For the mat, I used brown cardstock and softened it using a mixture of white and a little brown acrylic paint applied with a roller (see page 92). This softens the brown and brings in the texture of the wall in the photograph. The girls chose the quotation for the page themselves.

Atmosphere

The key to creating atmosphere is choosing the right colours, techniques, texture of paper and embellishments to suit your photographs. For example, if you have a layout set in an historic city, you might choose colours that harmonise with the stonework. If you want to emphasise the formality of the buildings, you might arrange the photographs straight rather than at an angle. You can then add carefully chosen embellishments which have the look of that historical period (see pages 90–91, 'Venice'). If, on the other hand, you have a picture of a modern cityscape, you might choose metallic papers or use layers of acetate. Embellishments in this case would be simple and bold. If a day on a farm is your theme, corrugated paper or suede combined with gingham, raffia or string will give a rustic feel. Torn edges and chalking or inking could also work well.

Outdoor fun

The children were in their element when we went to this water park in France for the day. A bright turquoise background unifies the layout because turquoise appears in all the photographs. The shade that I have chosen complements the colour of the water and water slides. As I wanted to include a lot of photographs, I limited the use of patterned paper to avoid making the layout too busy. The paper I used has a 'watery' feel. This layout is all about enjoyment and activity, so cutting the photographs into different shapes and arranging them at angles adds to the overall sense of vitality. All the embellishments are in keeping with the watery theme.

Stormy weather

These photographs were taken off the coast of Norway in a stormy week. I picked sombre colours to help to emphasise the stormy conditions, with just a hint of mustard yellow for the journaling. The yellow brings out the colours in the rainbow. I placed the photographs at an angle to give the impression that all is not calm! Two small matted maps cut from the holiday brochure locate the storm. I created the title using rub-on transfers which, being slightly textured and rough, add to the idea of rough seas. The gingham ribbon that forms a frame was lightly rubbed with an inkpad before it was attached. This helps to add to the stormy atmosphere.

Emphasis

There are many cropping techniques that you can use to emphasise certain aspects of your photographs. The shapes you crop, the embellishments you add, even the arrangement of your pictures together contribute to the overall 'message' of the page.

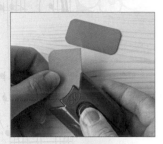

Use a corner punch to create bricks from rectangles of paper in shades of brown.

Hadrian's Wall

This is a simple page using some old walking photographs. To emphasise the idea of the wall, I have built one from cardstock scraps!

A pair of fancy-edged scissors will give your matting interesting and unusual edges. They are available in many different designs.

Tree climbing

At my in-laws' house there was an old tree that the children used to enjoy climbing. I have turned the photographs of them doing this into a tree shape by cutting them into circles of different sizes, matting them on green cardstock and creating interesting edges using fancy-edged scissors.

Skiing in Zermatt

Six diamond shapes together make a snowflake, which is very appropriate for photographs of skiing. This is also a good way of fitting several photographs on a page.

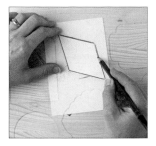

I held each photograph and a stencil up to the light to mark out the shape (see page 62). I then cut out each diamond with a craft knife and metal ruler.

Play

The motion of the swing is emphasised by the wavy edge that I cut into the pale green cardstock. Placing the photographs and the title at an angle also contributes to the sense of movement. I used a mixture of white, green and brown acrylic paint applied with a roller on the background cardstock. Using the same paint mix, I placed the cut letters on a rough piece of cardstock and simply rolled the paint over them. After they had dried, I stuck them to the layout.

Norfolk

Use your imagination when adding emphasis. Here the children wrote the title on the beach with stones, which I then photographed! The strips of mosaic at the top and bottom of this page capture aspects of our Norfolk holiday.

69

Playfulness

Robert enjoyed peering through the yellow rings in the play area. The layout emphasises this by replicating the rings. Although the photograph was taken on a dull day, the page colours help to 'lift' it – red to match Robert's trousers, yellow for the rings and green to tie in with the background. Using blocks of colour is an easy way to create a unified layout.

Katie and Martin

Here I focused on Katie's round earrings and skirt which are both black polka dot. I cut a large circle from the background tan cardstock and placed polka dot paper behind. Note that inking the edges of the cardstock titles helps them to stand out. This technique is demonstrated on page 78.

Plum picking

I have enlarged a photograph of plum trees and used that as a frame for the images of pigs in an orchard. A rustic feel is created by choosing a textured card for the background, using rub-on paint along its edges and framing the title in brown cardstock.

Painting & decorating

The pale pink cardstock has been distressed using sandpaper, an effect that links the background to the photographs and to the overall theme of decorating a bedroom. The photographs have also been sanded and the title was painted on using foam stamps, as if with emulsion.

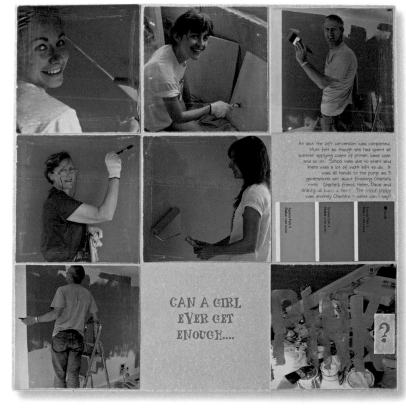

Techniques

The wonderful thing about scrapbooking is that you can use a limitless range of techniques on your pages. All you need to keep in mind is the message you are trying to convey, but beyond that there are no rules! I never cease to be amazed at how unique and individual each scrapbooker's style is.

Frames: Views of Bath

The right frame will make your photograph stand out on the page. If your design contains more than one photograph, framing will create a focal point. The type of frame you use will contribute to the overall mood of the page. For example, 'Annie the Bridesmaid' (see page 75) has a formal look while James jumping through a triangular frame (see page 77) is fresh and active.

This frame is easy to make and can be adapted to suit many projects. Simply change the proportions of the frame and experiment with different ways of decorating the card that you have used.

You will need

Photographs

Dark green cardstock,
30.5 x 30.5cm (12 x 12in)

Two sheets of apple-green cardstock,
30.5 x 30.5cm (12 x 12in)

Patterned paper,
30.5 x 30.5cm (12 x 12in)

Sheet of vellum

Craft knife and cutting mat

Metal ruler

Photo tabs

Double-sided tape

Hole punch

Rubber stamp and gold inkpad

Green brad

Ribbon

Eight green eyelets and eyelet tool kit

Lime green acrylic paint

Paper piercer

Sticker machine (optional)

Pen or computer

1. Measure out four rectangles for your frame on cardstock and cut them out. Make sure that they are long enough to overlap each other at the corners.

72

2. Cut the corners off the top and bottom of the two short sections of the frame. Line up each end with the grid on your cutting mat and slice the corner off diagonally.

3. Use photo tabs to attach the short sections of the frame to the long sections. Place the frame on a piece of scrap paper and stamp all over it using a rubber stamp. Stamp over the edges as shown.

4. Use double-sided tape to fix your photograph to the back of the frame. Use the hole punch from the eyelet tool kit to make two holes at the top and thread ribbon through. To attach your frame to the page, make a hole using a paper piercer as shown.

5. Attach a brad and tie the ends of the ribbon around it. Use photo tabs to stick your frame in the desired position on the page.

The finished layout. I built it up using more photographs and patterned paper. For the title, 'Bath', I used lime green acrylic paint on vellum and it over a photograph using eyelets. The journaling and smaller titles were created on the computer, then stuck over green card using a sticker machine.

Frames 2: Annie the Bridesmaid

This frame is simple to make but gives a sophisticated finish. Essentially it is a covered frame. Once you have mastered the technique, you can make similar frames of any size and cover them in whatever paper suits your page.

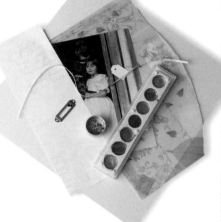

You will need

Photograph

Cream cardstock,
30.5 x 30.5cm (12 x 12in)

Cardstock for the frame,
30.5 x 30.5cm (12 x 12in)

Vellum,
30.5 x 30.5cm (12 x 12in)

Patterned paper,
30.5 x 30.5cm (12 x 12in)

Ribbon

Tiny white tag

Marker pen

Metallic rub-on paints

White rub-on transfers

Metal bookplate

Five small metallic brads

Glue stick

Metal ruler

Craft knife and cutting mat

Photo tabs

Pencil

Pen or computer

Paper piercer

Leaf skeletons

1. First measure your photograph to determine the size of the frame. The inside of the frame needs to be slightly smaller than the photograph you are framing. Use a pencil and ruler to measure out your complete frame on a piece of cardstock.

2. Cut the frame out using a craft knife and metal ruler.

3. Place your patterned paper face down on a cutting mat. Use glue stick to glue the frame to the paper. Now cut around the frame leaving a margin that is slightly less than the width of the frame.

4. Cut around the inside of the frame leaving a smaller margin and remove the paper rectangle that cutting creates. Now cut off each corner at a diagonal, leaving a small space between the frame and the cut, as shown.

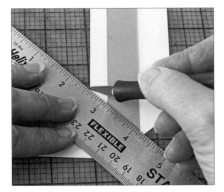 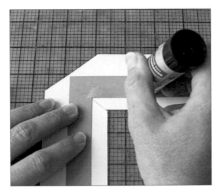 

5. Cut a diagonal line at each corner on the inside of the frame, taking care not to cut through the frame.

6. Spread glue over the frame. This gives a neater result than trying to put glue on the paper.

7. Fold over the inner paper edges first, then the outer paper edges. Smooth them all down. Attach the frame to your photograph using photo tabs and build your scrapbooking page. To attach a sheet of vellum, make holes with a paper piercer (see page 73) and then add the brads. Embellish the page using text, a metal bookplate, ribbon, rub-on transfers and a tag.

The finished layout. I added a tiny tag with the words 'Aged 4' and gave it a vintage feel using rub-on metallic paints. Rub-on transfers were used to create the word 'dream'. The journaling was typed on a computer, and leaf skeletons were added for a delicate touch.

I love this very wistful photograph of Annie. I framed it to enhance the feeling of her looking out of the church door and used pale, softly coloured paper and vellum for a romantic look.

(Page based on an idea by Karen McIvor of Scrapaholic Ltd)

Framing a detail

Framing a detail within the photograph rather than the picture itself is striking and unusual.

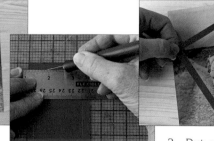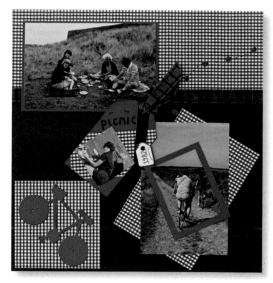

1. Measure the area of the photograph that you want to frame.

2. Draw the frame on to card and cut it out with a craft knife.

3. Put photo tabs on the pencilled side of the frame and position it over the photograph.

Picnic

Making a negative frame

Decide where to position your frame on the page before you start drawing and cutting. Remember that if you draw your frame on the right-hand side of the page, when you turn it over it will appear on the left-hand side.

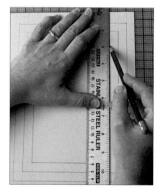

1. Measure your picture. Then draw three rectangles as shown, the smallest of which must be slightly smaller than your photograph.

2. Use a craft knife and metal ruler to cut round your rectangles. Discard the larger frame, fix decorative paper under the 'hole' and fix the picture and smaller frame in place using photo tabs.

Sisters

Fixing a frame with eyelets, snaps or brads

This frame is simplicity itself: four strips of card fixed in place with either eyelets, snaps or brads. It looks casual here with overlapping edges, but if each strip was lined up straight, it would look more formal.

1. Cut out two long and two short strips of card. Arrange them in the shape of a frame over the photograph on your page. I have also placed mesh underneath the photograph here.

2. Fix the photograph to the mesh using photo tabs. Now hammer in a snap at each corner using tools from your eyelet kit.

Eyes

Making a triangular frame

A triangular frame emphasises action. Measure your photograph first as your frame needs to be as big as, or slightly bigger than, the picture.

1. Draw a diagonal line down the length of your cardstock.

2. Position a protractor at the end of the line and mark a 60° angle.

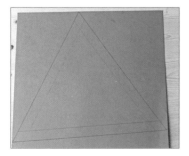

3. Draw in the second line at a 60° angle, then complete the triangle. Draw a smaller triangle inside this one, according to the size of frame you need. Cut out the frame with a craft knife and slip it over the picture.

James

Effects

There are all kinds of exciting visual effects that you can use on your projects. Again, the trick is to pick effects that are appropriate for the scrapbook page in question.

Double-sided tape and beads

Beads are available in all the colours of the rainbow and if you match them well to your theme, they can add a fun twist to your page. Clear or blue/green beads are ideal for seaside or poolside pictures.

1. Place double-sided tape in the area where you want beads. Peel off the backing.

2. Simply shake beads evenly over the double-sided tape. Shake off the excess.

Take time every day to be silly

Inking and sanding

You can ink the edges of photographs, mats or entire pieces of cardstock.
Inking adds dimension to the page and can produce an aged look.
Sanding also ages paper, tones down strong patterns and creates texture.

Pull an inkpad along the edge of your card or paper. Inking the card in this way adds subtle definition to the edges.

Gently remove the surface of patterned paper using grade three sandpaper.

Belton House

Tearing and chalking

Tearing paper or photographs creates a rough edge which can then be chalked to blend in with your page. This works well with seaside and snow scenes.

1. Tear the edge of the photograph slowly towards you.

2. Use a cotton wool pad to rub a little chalk in to the torn edge.

Glue and thread

Thread adds interest and texture. Here the threads mimic the rays of the sun and also cover each join where two pieces of different coloured card meet.

1. Use a fine-tip glue applicator to add a line of glue along the join.

2. Press your decorative thread on to the glue.

Summer in the South of France

Embossing

Embossing adds a richness to your page that is perfect for a wedding theme but take care not to overdo it – it can be garish. The powder is available in a variety of thicknesses and colours.

1. Press the stamp into an embossing inkpad and stamp along the edge of your card.

2. Scatter embossing powder over the stamped area. Shake off the excess powder and return it to the pot.

3. Hold a heating tool over the stamped area and the powder will melt. Leave to cool.

> *WARNING Heating tools get extremely hot. Keep your hands away from the heat source. If in doubt, use tweezers to hold the card. Work on a heat-proof surface.*

Katie

The title was created on an ink-jet printer and embossed before the ink dried.

Annie snorkelling

This was Annie's first experience of flippers. They were far too big! I have enhanced the beach theme by adding sand and acrylic paint to the page. The title was made from stickers which were painted over and then removed. The technique is explained on page 84.

Family Malden

I have used traditional colours and an old-fashioned font style to enhance the heritage theme. Embossed paper seemed appropriate for the period feel and I used rub-on paints to age it. The names and dates on the strips identify the people in the picture and give the page a personal touch. The smallest boy on the table is my Dad! Note that the heritage photograph has not been cropped.

Me!

One method of adding extra texture is by crumpling the paper or card before you sand it. Here the red strips and mats have been crumpled into a ball, smoothed out and then sanded with grade three sandpaper. The background cardstock was also lightly sanded to make the overall look less formal. If you want to create an aged look, you can ink lightly over the sanded card with an inkpad. You can attach the crumpled card to your pages as it is or, if you want to make it flatter, iron the reverse of the cardstock using your iron's lowest setting.

(Page based on an idea by Karen McIvor of Scrapaholic Ltd. Photograph by Touch Studios)

Jump

I cut the photographs into arbitrary shapes and stuck the pieces on in a random arrangement at lots of different angles. This is a variation of the slicing technique shown on page 82. It gives an impression of movement. I embossed the background cardstock and the hand-cut title with snowflakes to underline the wintery theme.

Slicing: At the Seaside

Slicing is a technique that I use often. You cut two or more different photographs into segments and arrange the segments so that your pictures are interleaved. It is very simple technique but the results are dramatic. Before you begin, decide on the focal point of your picture and then slice off segments from either side. They can be cut evenly, unevenly or a mixture of both. You will find that slicing draws attention to the action in your photograph whilst giving your page an overall sense of liveliness and movement.

When my girls were little, we spent many summer holidays in Norfolk. For this project I wanted to create a visual representation of happy days on the beach. The 'touchy-feely' embellishments help the memory process, especially the shells which were collected at the time.

You will need

Photographs

Two sheets of pale blue cardstock, 30.5 x 30.5cm (12 x 12in)

Brown cardstock, 30.5 x 30.5cm (12 x 12in)

Cream cardstock for matting, 30.5 x 30.5cm (12 x 12in)

Two sheets of sand style patterned paper, 30.5 x 30.5cm (12 x 12in)

Craft knife and cutting mat

Trimmer

Double-sided tape

Photo tabs

Metal-rimmed tag

Shell rubber stamp and inkpad

Acetate

Computer or pen

'Summer' rub-on transfer

Fine string

Eight eyelets and eyelet tool kit

Four metallic brads

Sand, glue and foam roller

Netting

Shells

1. Select photographs that complement each other. In this case, three pictures of a similar view each taken at a different distance.

2. A trimmer or small guillotine will give you crisp, straight edges. Slice off segments at each side of the picture's focal point.

3. Reassemble your photographs on your work surface. This will make it easier to decide how best to interleave the segments.

4. Mat the segment featuring your focal point, then take time experimenting with the arrangement of your other segments on your work surface. Once you are completely happy with the design, fix them to your pages using photo tabs.

5. Build up your page using a range of effects and embellishments. Here I applied glue along the bottom of the page using a foam roller and sprinkled sand on it. I placed a stamped seashell stamp behind my journaling and added shells and netting. The netting is fixed to the back of the page using double-sided tape without removing the backing. The title is a rub-on transfer.

6. You can pick out a detail on your page using a frame made from a metal-rimmed tag. Using a craft knife, cut a cross into the tag as shown. Cut right the way up to each corner.

7. Push your finger through the middle of the cross and then carefully pull out each triangle of card. Glue the metal frame over your chosen detail.

8. A string frame is another way to add emphasis. Make four eyelet holes to thread the string through and stick each length at the back of the photograph as for the netting in step 5.

The finished layout. Interleaving segments of different photographs allows you to play with scale. For example, the groynes on the beach are exaggerated because they are cut from close-up photographs.

Silhouetting: The Sandcastle

Silhouetting means cutting away distracting backgrounds to leave your subject matter in silhouette, as the name suggests. It is an exceptionally useful technique. Along with removing unwanted areas of the picture, silhouetting also creates a slightly three-dimensional effect, creating album pages that really leap out at you. It is ideal for presenting a lot of photographs of one event, such as a party or gathering. Sometimes you are able to make an entirely new picture from your photographs using this technique.

Annie was very proud of her sandcastle! I wanted her sitting on the sandcastle to be the main focus of the picture. The two people standing directly behind her head were distracting, so I chose to silhouette the photograph.

You will need

Photographs

Turquoise cardstock, 30.5 x 30.5cm (12 x 12in)

Sand cardstock, 30.5 x 30.5cm (12 x 12in)

White acrylic paint

Paint brush

Letter stickers

Starfish rubber stamp and inkpad

Dark-coloured inkpad

Photo tabs

Scissors

Glue stick

Tag craft punch

Hole punch

Raffia

1. Roughly tear the bottom off a piece of sand-coloured cardstock and stick it to your page using photo tabs. Add the title using letter stickers.

2. Loosely paint over the lettering with acrylic paint. Leave until nearly dry.

3. Carefully peel off each letter.

4. Cut closely around the edge of the detail that you wish to feature. Tuck the photograph under the sand-coloured card and then fix to the page using photo tabs.

5. Build up your page using another matted picture and effects such as stamping. In this case, a starfish is perfect for the theme.

6. Tags add interest to any page and here a tag draws attention to the top of the sandcastle. I printed the text on to card with the computer and then punched out the shape.

7. Use a hole punch to make a hole at the top of the tag and feed through a raffia tie. Ink the edges of the tag in a dark colour (see page 78) to give it extra definition.

Tip

Silhouetting seems simple but it is surprisingly easy to get it wrong. Two general points: always cut very close to the image when you are creating the silhouette. If you leave too much space around it, it will appear to float when you place it on the page. If you are silhouetting pictures of people, you will find that arms and legs often go out of frame in a photograph. Cover up these 'ends' with other elements on your page.

The finished page

Lettering

Recording memories is as much the purpose of scrapbooking as displaying photographs. Adding an eye-catching title and some journaling really helps to capture the feeling or moment that you want to record on your scrapbook page. Various methods of creating interesting letters and numbers for titles are described below. Hopefully you will be inspired to adapt the ideas to make numerous examples of your own!

Covering letters with collage

Collage works best with large letters as they give you the room to include lots of photographs. I tend to use them as the first letter in a title and complete the word with printed, painted or sticker letters.

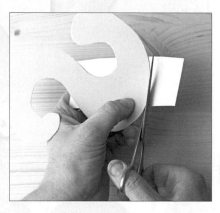

1. Draw a letter on to card and cut it out. Fix a small section of photograph to the letter using photo tabs.

2. Trim off the excess photograph, following the shape of the letter. Work your way around the letter adding and trimming different sections of photograph.

S for spring

You can trim around the shape of a detail in your picture, as I have here with the blossom, to give a layered effect.

Using stencils and stickers

Using one long sticker across the length of your title gives it impact and adds interest to your page.

1. Stick a decorative sticker to a piece of card.

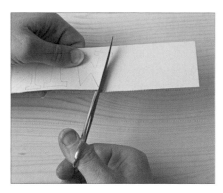

3. Carefully cut out each letter with a pair of sharp scissors.

2. Turn the piece of card over and, using a letter stencil face down, draw round the letters you require. Spell out the word from right to left.

Winter

When you turn each letter over you will find that the sticker has created an interesting pattern across the length of your word.

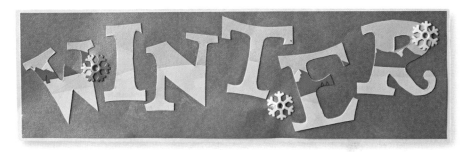

Shadow letters or numbers

This is another fun way to use a stencil but you need to cut neatly for this one!

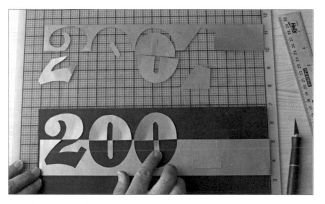

1. Using the stencil face down, draw your letters or numbers on the back of a piece of gold paper. Use a craft knife to cut round each letter but do not pull them away from the paper. Instead, cut a line straight across the middle of the paper holding the cork-backed metal ruler down firmly.

2. Place the bottom section of gold paper on to cardstock and gently remove all parts of the numbers. Line up the top half of each number with the hole left by the bottom half. When you are happy with the positioning, fix with photo tabs.

2004

I used a star stamp and gold ink to create a subtle pattern on the background card. The title could be used for a New Year or Review of the Year page.

Cutting numbers or letters from a photograph

Before you begin, carefully consider where you are going to position your numbers or letters. Holding the photograph up to the light may help you decide (see page 62).

1. Put your stencil face down on the back of the photograph and draw round the relevant number with a pencil.

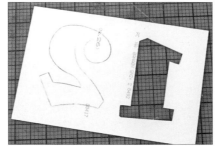

2. Use a craft knife to cut out the number on a cutting mat.

3. Mat your number and stick it back over the hole that it left in your photograph using photo tabs. Matting has two advantages; it adds definition and also covers up any evidence of cutting on the photograph itself.

Photo sandwich

Making a title with a photo sandwich using the same colour card as your background is a great way to co-ordinate your title with your page.

1. Glue a strip of card across the top and bottom of a photograph but do not cover all of the picture. For added texture and interest one piece of card could be cut and the other torn.

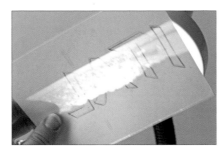

I have used colours that complement the photograph, but you could use the colours of a country's flag.

2. Turn the photograph over and stencil letters on the back, remembering to work from right to left. Holding the photograph up to the light will help you judge where to position the letters. Cut the letters out and remount them on your page.

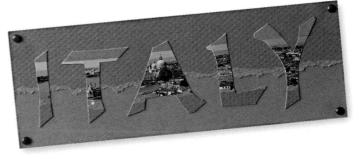

Using a detail from a photograph

This creative technique visually links the title to the photographs on the rest of the page. Some shapes lend themselves to certain letters: any tall structure or even a person can make an effective 'I'.

Cut out a detail that suggests a particular letter shape from a photograph. Build up the rest of the word using an alternative method of lettering.

Using computer fonts

Fonts can be printed straight on to card from a home computer and there is a vast and inspiring array of font styles available.

Select a font you like and adjust the size on screen. Use the 'rotate' and 'flip' functions to reverse your text (or refer to the instructions for reversing text with your software) and print it on to cardstock. Then cut each letter out by hand. This avoids the lines showing on the front.

Using a die cut machine

A die cut machine creates instant, professional-looking lettering. You can use the 'empty' negative cut letter shapes as well as the positive letters the machine stamps out as part of your page.

To cut out a letter, slip the card or photograph into the machine, place a letter block over it and under the handle barrier and press down hard.

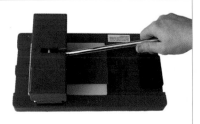

Decorative punching

If you are involved in other crafts such as card making, you may already have to hand many of the craft tools used in scrapbooking. Decorative craft punches are particularly versatile and useful to scrapbookers. A well-chosen punch can add the perfect touch to your page that will really bring out your theme. You can use the positive or negative image made by a punch and you may choose to punch through card, paper or even photographs.

Positive shapes

Punches are available in many designs so you should be able to find something appropriate to your theme. Simply place your card, paper or photograph in the punch and press down. Glue the resulting shape on to your work.

Negative shapes

You can also experiment with the negative shapes that punches leave behind. Try creating a decorative edge (see 'Forever'), or punching a row of the same design.

Impressions of Venice

In order to capture as many of the different scenes in this lovely city as possible, I decided to make a photographic mosaic (see pages 94–95). The design of the punch seems in keeping with Venetian architecture and mosaics are found all over the city. The two techniques combined contribute to the sense of place.

1. Turn a large square punch upside-down and place your photograph in it facing towards you. Position the detail in the square and push down hard to punch it out.

2. Use a small craft punch on paper matching your background cardstock.

3. Use a trimmer or guillotine to cut a square around your decorative punching. Then incorporate your punched pieces of card into the design.

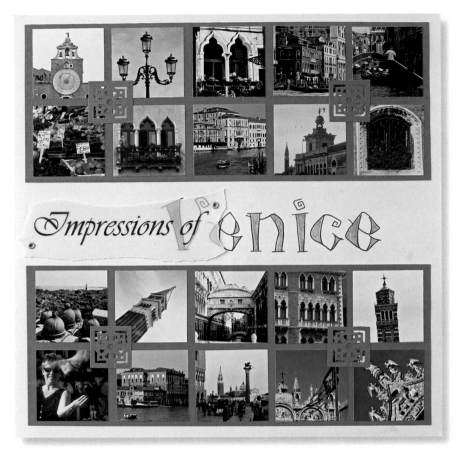

The finished layout. As well as focusing on details of the city, punched out photographs allow you to fit quite a number on a page, creating a vivid impression of the place.

Emma's bedroom

I have made a frame around two photographs of Emma's bedroom. The punched shapes stuck on to the frame help to emphasise that it is a child's bedroom.

Montage: Pool Matters

Montage is exciting because you can use any combination of cutting techniques to achieve the effect you want. The only limit is your imagination! It is a great means of fitting many different photographs on one page or layout, and the finished montage becomes a whole new picture in its own right.

I wanted this layout to celebrate happy days round a pool on a summer holiday. I had lots of photos to include so I cropped them to focus on the people. Cutting out circles adds to the theme of water and a random arrangement on the layout gives an active feel which complements the photographs. Note that I enlarged some of the photographs to give them extra punch.

You will need

Two sheets of 30.5 x 30.5cm (12 x 12in) turquoise cardstock

Teal cardstock, 30.5 x 30.5cm (12 x 12in)

Turquoise vellum, 30.5 x 30.5cm (12 x 12in)

White cardstock, 30.5 x 30.5cm (12 x 12in)

Cutting mat

Scissors

Three white eyelets

Eyelet tool kit

Clear plastic adhesive pebbles

Rub-on transfers

Turquoise acrylic paint (in two shades of turquoise)

Textured paste

Foam roller

Circle cutters and blades

Photo tabs

Palette or old plate

1. Squeeze some acrylic colour into textured paste on a palette or old plate. This paste contains tiny clear beads which adds to the watery theme.

2. Mix the colour and the textured paste using a foam roller.

3. Roll the textured paint mix across your page in a loose, wave-like movement. Wash out your roller straight after use.

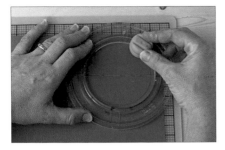

4. Place teal cardstock on a cutting mat and position a circle cutter on top. Pull the blade around the circle, holding it against the plastic. Use the same technique to cut more circles from card or vellum and to cut out details from your photographs. Vary the size of circle cutter that you use.

5. To create a 3D sticker, peel the backing off a clear plastic adhesive pebble and stick it on to the front of a photograph off-cut. Trim around it. Make several 3D stickers in this way to glue on to your page.

6. Use rub-on transfers to add text to your card circles and then attach the circles to your page with eyelets, using the eyelet tool kit.

I attached the photographs and vellum with photo tabs. Since tabs show through vellum, I slipped the vellum under the photographs so that they were hidden. The plastic pebbles can be strategically positioned to hold down vellum, too. I created the word 'Pool' for the title using the technique described on page 88. Note that the photographs cross over the break between the two pages so that the whole layout is unified.

Mosaics

Mosaics are simple and satifisfying to make and they create something entirely new from well-loved photographs. It is best to start off with squares and rectangles but once you feel inspired you can use all manner of shapes.

2003

This is a random selection of 'left over' photos from 2003. I started from the outside of the layout and worked inwards, filling any gaps with text and embellishments. It was easy work – just one evening in front of the television!

Using templates to start a mosaic

Before you start to cut up your photographs, it is a good idea to work out exactly how many squares and rectangles you need for your mosaic. The simplest way to do this is to cut out squares and rectangles from scrap paper and experiment with positioning them on the page. Then use your scrap paper arrangement as a guide as you cut and position your photographs.

Kephalonia

This is a simple but beautiful mosaic that allows the pictures to speak for themselves. I cut the two main photographs into six equally-sized squares and used a small square craft punch to make squares for the border. You can adapt this design to any theme.

1. Use a square punch to cut out as many squares of card and photograph as you need to create a border around the edge of your card. As you arrange the squares, try to give a random feel to the pattern, varying light and dark squares and spreading out coloured squares. Repositionable tape will allow you to adjust and refine the arrangement as you work and help you to create an even mosaic.

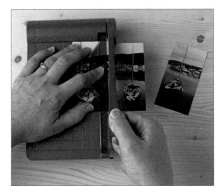

2. Using a trimmer, slice your main photograph into six equal parts. Repeat with another favourite photograph. Reassemble the pictures within the border and finally add a line of mosaic squares across the middle.

The finished page. I typed the title on the background cardstock using an A3 printer. I assembled the mosaic as shown, trimmed the cardstock after assembly and double-mounted it before attaching the whole picture to the background using photo tabs. Embellishments formed the finishing touch.

For my best friend, Victoria, who got me into all this in the first place!

Eyelets for Scrapbooks

Sarah McKenna

Introduction

I started to create scrapbooks in 1997 following a visit to the States. I had always been a keen photographer and, with a large family, produced lots of photographs. Scrapbooking supplied a means of creating meaningful family albums and it was not long before my children were creating albums with me.

Once the basic cropping techniques have been mastered, scrapbookers usually want to start adding embellishments to their pages. The versatile eyelet kit then becomes an essential tool. Once you have started using eyelets, you will wonder how you ever scrapbooked without them!

In this section I aim to take you through the many uses of eyelets. I start with their essential attributes: for attaching vellum, acetate and fabric to your pages, without any risk of glue showing through and spoiling your project and with the added benefit of providing charming detail. I will then show you how you can use eyelets to add a range of other embellishments and accents including frames, mini-books, clasps, tags, charms and more. Eyelets come in a range of designs including letters, words and tiny replicas of items so that you can add detail and provide emphasis to your pages.

I hope you will be inspired by the ideas in this section so that you, too, believe that the eyelet tool kit was the best scrapbooking investment you ever made!

simple **FUN**

WIFE

MUS

Sharing
Surprises
Joy Best Wish
special gift
good
PHOTO friendship

LOVER
MOTHER
SCRAPBOOKER create
PHOTOGRAPHER
HOMEMAKER

Winter

Sledging

On the evening of 27 January 2004, it
snowed heavily. We woke the next morning
to a winter wonderland and to more excitement
on the radio that school was closed. Martin
couldn't get to work either. It was Kate's
birthday so we got the sledges and dog and
walked up through the woods into the valley
playing up there on the sledges. The children
played for ages on the sledges in the meadow
and Louise produced lots of warm drinks and
flapjack. I think it was a perfect 13th birthday
for Kate.

Materials

Scrapbooking allows you to preserve your photographs and your memories. One of its great strengths is that everyone can develop their own scrapbooking style, linked to their interests in other crafts, such as painting, sewing, beading and stamping. The materials that can be used for scrapbooking are therefore almost infinite. However, as the craft is about preserving as well as displaying and recording, it is important that all materials which will touch your photographs are acid free, otherwise photographs can deteriorate, spoiling your scrapbooks. It is best to buy materials from reliable scrapbook sources and to check the labels to see that they are of archival quality, photo safe or acid free.

A guillotine large enough to cut scrapbooking cardstock.

Basic equipment

You do not actually need a lot to get started. The basics consist only of albums and paper or card and cutting, sticking and recording materials.

A **guillotine** capable of cutting 30.5 x 30.5cm (12 x12in) card – the basic scrapbooking size – is helpful for cutting card and paper neatly and quickly. A smaller **trimmer** or **guillotine** is useful for smaller pieces of card and for photographs.

Scissors are essential. I use a very small sharp pair for close cropping work.

A **craft knife** allows you to cut very accurately, for example for hand-cut titles or where precise measurements are important such as for mosaics. It is used with a **cork-backed metal ruler** (to prevent slipping) and a **self-healing cutting mat**. My mat is slightly larger than a 30.5 x 30.5cm (12 x12in) scrapbook page and is ideal. It also has measurements marked on it which prove very useful. The cutting mat is also essential for use with the various **cutting tools** available, such as **circle** and **oval cutters**. A **wavy ruler** is fun for different cutting effects – see the last project in this book.

Adhesives come in many guises and you will probably need a variety for different purposes. **Double-sided photo tabs** and **tape** are useful for adhering cardstock, paper and photographs. **Glue pens** and **water-based adhesive** are useful for attaching embellishments. Use **glue dots** for the heavier ones. Regular **PVA glue** or **glue stick** are good when making items from cardstock, such as covering frames. **Repositionable adhesive** (available in a runner) is invaluable for attaching items temporarily that you might want to move later, for example in mosaic and collage work.

A cutting mat, mini guillotine, circle cutters, eraser, wavy ruler, pens and gel pens, coloured and graphite pencils, cork-backed metal ruler, photo-safe wax crayons, craft knife, embossing tool, scissors, PVA glue, glue pen, glue stick, photocare solution and pad, tweezers, photo tabs, double-sided tape, repositionable adhesive on a runner and glue dots.

Pens, **pencils** and **crayons** can help to make your pages really distinctive and are great for adding that personal touch. My favourites are fine-tipped marker pens. **Graphite pencils** are useful for measuring and drafting journaling or titles and can be rubbed out later with an ordinary **eraser**. I find **computer fonts** invaluable for journaling and titles too. I use them when I want a more 'published' look.

A **photo-safe wax crayon** is helpful for marking cutting lines on photographs which can be rubbed out later using a cloth. Finally, when I have completed a page, I always go over the photographs with a **photocare solution** and cloth before placing it in the album. This removes any fingerprints and sticky marks.

Albums, cardstock and paper

Albums need to be acid free. They come in a variety of sizes: 30.5 x 30.5cm (12 x12in) is the most popular, and all the projects in this section are for this size. Another standard size is 21.5 x 28cm (8.5 x11in), but this is not so popular in the UK. Smaller sizes: 20.3 x 20.3cm (8 x 8in) and 15.2 x 15.2cm (6 x 6in) are also available and are nice as gift albums.

The type of album I find the easiest to work with is called a **top-loading album.** All finished layouts are loaded into page protectors, which are then secured in an album, usually on metal posts. I find these **post-bound albums** the easiest. You can rearrange the finished pages in any order you like and add extra pages, so that you don't have to work chronologically. **Strap-bound albums** are also popular. With these you work straight on to the page but you can remove pages from the album to work on or to rearrange them. The pages are fixed to straps in the album.

Paper comes in varying thicknesses, colours and designs. The main thing is to ensure that it is acid and lignin free. Lignin causes the paper to go brown and crumble. The thicker 30.5 x 30.5cm (12 x 12in) paper is called **cardstock** and usually forms a sturdy background to any layout. Thinner paper and card is often used to provide added interest and enhance pages. There is a whole variety of designs and what each person chooses will be determined by the layout being created and individual taste. When using patterned paper, make sure it doesn't detract from your photographs, which you usually want to be the main focus of a page. There are also some lovely **speciality papers** available, such as **vellum** and **textured paper** or **mesh**, which can be used to create more individual effects. This book shows how to attach these using eyelets.

Acetate

I absolutely love this! Sheets of acetate come with pre-printed colour or plain black designs and are wonderful for adding depth to a page. They come in a variety of sizes and often include words, sayings or thoughts which can help you to convey a message or emotion on your layout. You can also print your own journaling on acetates. I think that eyelets are the best way of attaching acetate to the page.

Eyelet tool kit

This kit is used to fix eyelets to your scrapbook pages. The method is demonstrated on pages 106 and 107. It is possible to fix as many as six layers of paper, cardstock or photographs with the standard 3mm (¹/₈in) eyelet.

The **hole punch** makes holes in paper or cardstock. It is possible to attach different heads to make different sized holes, depending on the size of eyelet chosen for the particular project.

The **hammer** is used to hammer the hole punch through the work.

The **setter** is used with the hammer to 'set' the eyelet in the hole.

The **setting mat** is used with all eyelet work to avoid making holes in your work surface! It is not vital to have a separate mat. I use the back of my self-healing cutting mat which I find more convenient for larger pieces of work, preserving the front of the mat for when I need to cut or measure.

The **piercing tool** is essential for removing paper debris from the hole punch. It is also extremely useful for marking out measured holes before punching and for pre-making holes to attach other items, such as brads or beads.

Other types of eyelet tool kit

There are a number of other eyelet tool kits now on the market. They all work on the same principle, which is to make a hole in the papers and to set the eyelet. One I have tried uses a twisting motion and another a spring action, instead of hammering. The type chosen is a matter of individual choice. I find the one featured here simple and effective – especially for getting through a number of layers. It is noisy, however, because of the hammering.

Eyelets and charms

Eyelets are one of the most versatile embellishments for scrapbooks but also have a practical use: they are extremely sturdy and are idcal for fastening vellum, acetate and fabrics where glue might show through. They are wonderful for providing a means of hanging or threading fibres, ribbon and other embellishments.

They come in an almost endless variety of shapes and three basic sizes: 1mm (1/16in), 3mm (1/8in) and the larger, or shaped, eyelets in 4mm (3/16in). I find the most useful size is the standard round 3mm (1/8in), in every colour of the rainbow! These are the ones I use most frequently. However, it is also possible to purchase eyelets with slightly longer or even very long stems. These are excellent if you want to fix a number of pieces of paper and card together, for example when making a tag or mini-book.

In addition to fixing together paper and related products, eyelets can also be used to attach charms. These range from letters to shapes, metal-rimmed tags, bookplates and a whole selection of metal hinges. Eyelets are ideal for attaching all of these firmly to layouts. Together with the charms, they add texture and dimension to layouts, which help to make them more interesting. The tiny 1mm (1/16in) eyelets can add charming detail to intricate embellishments but are fiddly to work with.

There is a whole range of eyelets in different shapes, from stars and flowers to animals and trinkets. In addition to having a practical function, these also help to add emphasis to layouts (see pages 130–135).

Eyelets can also be found with letters, words or phrases, which help to provide or add impact to journaling on a page.

Embellishments

These are the equivalent of the icing on the cake! The number of embellishments now available for scrapbook pages is enormous. It is tempting to use loads of them but I think they are best used sparingly to add a little finishing touch rather than to overwhelm the page. Some of the many available include:

Fibres, **thread**, **ribbons** and even **tinsel**! Great for hanging and threading charms, buttons, beads and tags. These are some of the most versatile embellishments for helping to add emphasis to the theme of a page. Depending on the choice, you can make your page feel rustic, using string or raffia, romantic, using pastel ribbons and highly decorated netting, seasonal, with tinsel or gold and silver threads, or masculine, with dark ginghams or leather thread.

Wires and chains Like fibre and ribbon, when used in conjunction with eyelets, these are useful for hanging things from and to add to the 'feel' of a page.

Fabric and **twill tape** have also become popular. It is possible to stamp and paint them and print on them using the computer.

Stickers, **feathers**, **beads**, **silk flowers**, **metal clasps** and **labels** can be used to add detail and emphasis.

Memorabilia Do not neglect your own tickets, tokens, cards, stamps, cigarette cards, leaflets, maps and other memorabilia. Not only do they add detail and dimension but they also make your pages truly personal. With the photographs, they are often the most interesting part of a scrapbook. It is best to spray memorabilia from an unknown source with archival mist before adhering them to your pages to ensure archival quality is preserved.

Slide mounts are very versatile as you can cover them in any paper to make them tone with your page. I prefer the card rather than plastic ones because you can punch holes in them (see page 114). They can be used to emphasise part of a photograph, highlight a word or frame another embellishment, or they can be made into individual shaker boxes.

A slide mount, ribbons, threads, tinsel, feathers, postage stamps, fabric and other stickers, cigarette cards, labels, a metal label, metal clasps, beads, silk flowers and a plug chain.

Other materials

Like embellishments, there is a huge variety of other materials available. What you use may depend largely upon what other crafts you enjoy.

Paint, acrylic and watercolour, **gesso** and **texture paste** can all create interesting additions to your pages. I frequently use them to paint backgrounds, using **brushes** and **foam rollers** in various designs for different effects. **Rub-on paints** are best applied with your finger and can be used for distressing, ageing or providing a rustic look on the layout.

Craft punches can be used to make a variety of shapes from paper, cardstock or photographs.

Rubber stamps, **foam stamps** and **inkpads** add detail to pages and can also be used for lettering. **Watermark stamp pads** can be used with stamps and chalks for a subtle background motif.

Chalks, **sandpaper** and **inks** are particularly useful to add age, texture and definition to a page.

Embossing powder and a **heating tool** can be used with an **embossing pen**, **pad** or stamps to add raised, textured detail to a page in a variety of finishes. You can create some stylish embellishments and the finished look has a wonderful texture and gloss. **Gold-** and **silver-leafing pens** can also be used for titles or the edges of cards. All of these are great for wedding or anniversary celebration pages and heritage.

Rub-on transfers, commonly in letter form, are great for creating words.

Adhesive remover is one of the most useful products around, and allows you to unstick anything without leaving marks should you change your mind.

I use a **protractor** to cut cardstock at precise angles, for example when making a triangular frame.

Letter or shape **stencils** are used for creating handwritten lettering or to make shapes from a particular paper or cardstock to coordinate with the layout.

Craft punches, foam and rubber stamps, walnut ink, embossing powder, rub-on transfers, a watermark stamp pad, sandpaper, dye inkpad, foam roller, protractor, rub-on paints, acrylic paints and paint brush, adhesive remover, stencil, heating tool, gold-leafing pen and stickers.

Techniques

One of the great advantages of using eyelets in your scrapbooks is the ease with which the technique of eyelet setting can be mastered. The technique remains the same whatever type of eyelet you choose for your scrapbook layout. I have used the tool kit demonstrated here for all the layouts in this book as I find it simple and effective, though the hammering makes it noisy. There are other types of kit available, as explained on page 102.

1. Always work on a setting mat or on the back of your cutting mat. This avoids making holes in your work surface or the measuring side of your cutting mat. Place the eyelet piercing tool where you want to put the eyelet in your layered card or paper. Tap the tool with the hammer reasonably hard. As a rough rule of thumb I usually say one tap of the hammer for each layer of paper you are trying to go through.

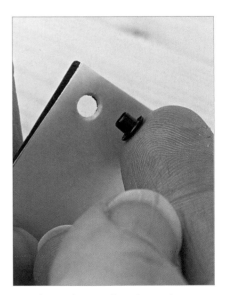

2. Place the eyelet through the hole.

3. Place the end of the setting tool in the back of the eyelet and tap it with the hammer. I usually tap the tool two or three times to set an eyelet.

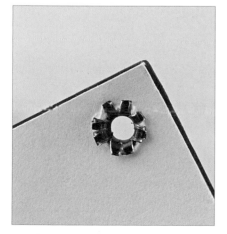

4. The setting tool presses open the back of the eyelet and fixes it in place.

The secured eyelet shown from the front.

Tip

The hole punch does have a tendency to become clogged with card and paper. I find the easiest way to clean it is to use the piercing tool to empty it.

Attaching vellum

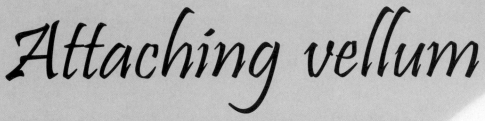

Vellum is a semi-transparent paper that is wonderful for adding dimension to scrapbook pages. It allows what is underneath to show through and sometimes provides a subtle or softening change of colour. It comes either plain (as in the 'Austria' example opposite) or coloured. Sometimes it is patterned as well – as in the other examples on these pages. Although vellum looks wonderful on layouts it can be really troublesome to fix because virtually every glue-based fixing product shows through, which spoils the effect. Eyelets are the answer! They not only solve this problem but also add dimension and detail of their own.

Sarah – bridesmaid

Given that this is a photograph of me (longer ago than I care to remember), I hesitate to call it 'heritage' style! However, that is the look I have gone for. The vellum incorporates a heritage-style design and I have enhanced the soft feel of the page by measuring out an inner frame, cutting it out with a craft knife and then tearing the inner edges. Heart-shaped eyelets complete the romantic feel.

Venice

Printed vellum has been used for the title on this page. I printed it on the computer and embossed it whilst the printing ink was still wet. Fixing the vellum over the photograph helps to give an impression of the place. The eyelets were chosen to complement the theme. Note that it is important to emboss the vellum before fixing it to the photograph, otherwise you might melt the photograph.

Austria

I drew and cut round a dinner plate to make the circle in the plain vellum and embossed the inner edge. Four eyelets fix the vellum to the page. The vellum map and crest were printed from the internet.

Dogs are just children with fur

A little bit of snow sends my dog into skittish mood! I have emphasised the snow in the photographs with the white spotted vellum. This has been fixed with red eyelets. Placing the title under the vellum and the embossed snowflake embellishment over it helps to add depth to the page.

Attaching acetate

Like vellum, acetate is a wonderfully versatile medium which allows you to add depth to a scrapbook page. Since it is completely transparent, anything placed underneath it will be more visible than when using vellum. Acetate comes pre-printed in a variety of sizes and designs. When words form part of the acetate's design, they can really help to emphasise the theme of the layout. Alternatively, you can use plain acetate and print your own journaling or titles using a computer.

For the 'Snow Day' layout, I printed the text on an A4 sheet of acetate using a number of different fonts. I cut a piece of watercolour paper to the same size and made pencil marks to indicate where the bands of colour should go, behind the lettering. I then painted the paper in my choice of colours, allowing the paint to dry before attaching the paper and then the acetate to the layout.

Snow day

When snow falls in the village where I live, it looks really beautiful. I had this photograph enlarged to 45.7 x 30.5cm (18 x 12in) and cut it to fit across two pages. The words printed on the acetate remind me of one of the lovely 'Snow Days' in 2004.

Emma

A 30.5 x 30.5cm (12x12in) acetate has been cut up to provide emphasis on two sides of the photograph, with paint and stamped motifs underneath adding to the theme. If the acetate contains a lot of wording it can overwhelm the photograph if placed on top. In these circumstances, the acetate can be more effective cropped, as here.

Play

By contrast, the whole acetate could be used here, as the wording is unobtrusive. Note that the blue printing picks out the colour of Annie's jacket, helping to make the layout coherent.

Attaching fabric

It is increasingly popular to use fabric and ribbon on scrapbook pages. They add texture and interest. However, as with vellum and acetate, attaching them with glue can prove hazardous because it shows through, particularly with mesh, gauze and fine ribbon. Eyelets are an ideal alternative and go through fabric easily.

1. Apply repositionable adhesive to the back of the twill tape.

2. Stick the tape on to the card to keep it taut. Then make a hole in it using the hammer and hole punching tool on a setting mat or the back of your cutting mat.

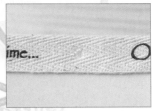

3. Do not worry if you cannot see a neat circular hole, as when piercing card or paper. The hole in the tape will hardly show, but it will be there nonetheless.

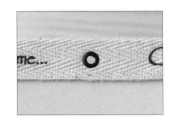

4. Push the eyelet in and set it in the usual way.

Once upon a time

A layout featuring all the family reading one relaxing summer holiday. The twill tape forms a binding and the layout opens out like a book. It can either be slipped into a page protector in its entirety and taken out to look at, or stuck with photo tabs on the outside of the page protector so that it is possible to open it out each time someone looks at the album.

Autumn

This is one of my favourite layouts in the book, evoking a misty, late autumn afternoon in the woods near my home. I replicated the soft feel of the photograph by subtle use of coloured ink sprayed on to the background card from a spray bottle. Sheer ribbon and mesh in autumn colours, attached with eyelets, enhance the theme. Note that it would not have been possible to use any form of glue on the ribbon or mesh without it showing through and spoiling the layout.

Hunt the washing pole

Ribbon has been attached to labels and journaling with enclosed eyelets (called snaps), and then the ribbon has been used to hang the labels from pegs on string, like a washing line.

Hanging & threading

If there is one thing that the eyelet was designed for, it is for hanging or threading and there is a whole range of materials that can be used for this purpose, from chains and wire to ribbon, string, twine and thread.

The technique shown below can be used to cover any size of card frame as well as slide mounts.

 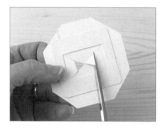  

1. Apply glue stick to the back of the slide mount and stick it to the paper. Use a craft knife to cut across the corners as shown and then cut a cross in the middle of the aperture.

2. Glue the front of the slide mount and snip off the points from the two triangular flaps that will cover the sides of the mount.

3. Fold back the edges of the paper and stick them down as shown.

4. Set an eyelet in the covered slide mount in the usual way and thread a length of plug chain through it.

Tip

The loose end of the chain slots into the fastener. This can be quite fiddly. The smaller the chain, the fiddlier it is. Make sure you use a chain that is small enough to fit through the eyelet.

It's the shades!

I have used the slide mounts and chains, patterned paper and embellishments to emphasise the theme of the page – the amazing psychedelic pink sunglasses that my children took to wearing for a couple of summers!

Stockings

The stocking opening ceremony is a big tradition in our family and with six of us it can take as long as two hours! I have made my own stocking tags using stickers and eyelets, and I have embossed the edges and hung them from festive gold fibre.

Adventure

Here I have threaded wire through eyelets and made journaling, photographs and titles into impromptu tags.

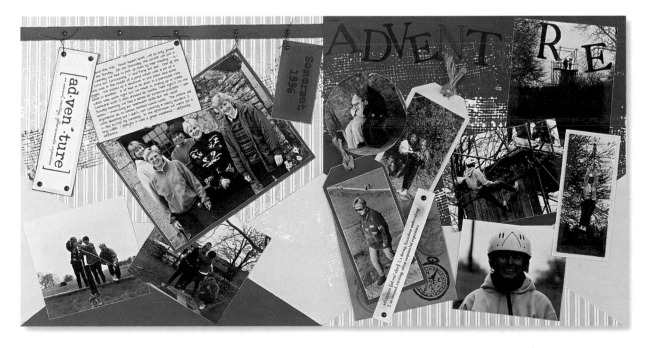

Lucy

Eyelets have been used for hanging both titles here but in different ways, one vertically and one horizontally.

On the farm

I have added a rustic feel to this layout by my choice of materials and techniques, including undyed string, ink and cork, and tearing and chalking photographs. The stamped background was made using a garden fern leaf dipped in acrylic paint and stamped on to the page.

Frames & borders

Eyelets are perfect for providing an eye-catching method of making frames and borders. They can be used with thread, string, ribbon, flax and fibres to highlight pages, journaling or individual photographs in a variety of ways.

2. Pierce holes and attach and set the eyelets in the usual way. Take your chosen thread and stick down the end on the back of the piece, then begin threading through the eyelets.

1. Draw a pencil line and mark the position of the eyelet holes with a piercing tool. Use an eraser to rub out the pencil line.

3. Continue threading the border in a shoelace pattern.

Sledging

This was a wonderful and unexpected day off school in 2004. We walked up through the woods to visit friends in the next valley and the children spent hours sledging. I have emphasised the fun and action by arranging the photographs at irregular angles and by adding the eyelet and fibre border. The red and yellow fibre coordinates with the colours in the photographs.

Simple fun

This is one of my favourite action shots. Nicholas spent a happy summer's afternoon bouncing on his trampoline for me and as his stance became more open, so did his smile! I did not want to over-complicate the page, as the photograph speaks for itself, so I have kept the design simple, like the title.

Giggle

For me, the photograph said it all. I wanted to keep it simple so the ribbon and eyelet border with its triangular cardstock corners just draws the eye into the photograph.

Charlie

This layout shows the subtle use of snaps. The four corners of the cardstock have been folded very lightly, so as not to crease the edge completely flat, and fixed with snaps in the corner. This is one of my favourite ways of framing a page or photograph, because it helps draw the eye into the layout. For this technique cardstock with different colours or patterns on each side works particularly well.

Emma – bridesmaid

In contrast to the 'Giggle' example on page 119, the eyelets here are placed just outside the photograph but still on the contrasting red cardstock mat. The gold string forms a very subtle frame and the eyelets along the green strip at the top of the layout provide a contrasting border.

Rest and relaxation

This is one of my favourite frames using eyelets. The four eyelets have been set into the actual photograph and string is threaded through the holes and knotted on the front of the layout, emphasising the focal point of the photograph. I have also added a tiny tag through one eyelet and an eyelet word.

Moreton Show

I created the central montage working from the outside edge inwards, overlaying some of the elements. I measured and spaced the eyelets for this border using the technique shown on page 118 and then threaded raffia through the eyelet holes for a rustic feel. I finished by using brown rub-on paint around the outer edge of the cardstock.

Impressions of Norway

Here I have created a border made entirely of ribbon, which has been threaded through four holes, one in each corner of the page, and fixed to the back of the layout using the technique shown on page 118. The outsized snowflake eyelets have been fixed into the same holes, helping to secure the ribbon.

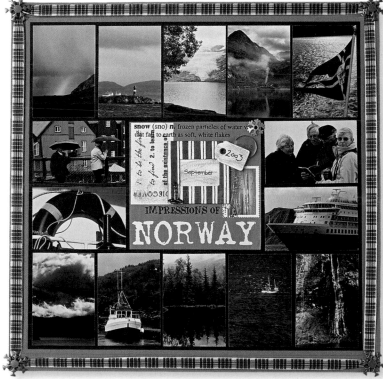

Mini-books

Mini-books have many uses. They are great for including a number of photographs where you have a lot from one event but do not want to create lots of individual layouts. They make perfect gifts – especially for birthdays or occasions such as Mother's Day. They are useful for including extra journaling – particularly if you have things to say that you would rather keep hidden from the casual viewer of your album!

This demonstration shows how to make a mini-book based on a cross design.

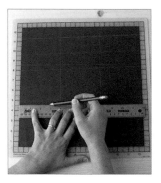

1. Mark out the cardstock into nine equal squares, each of sides 7.5cm (3in).

2. Cut out the corner squares.

3. Rub out the lines and fold in the sides.

4. Stick on the photographs and add any embellishments.

5. Measure, mark and make eyelet holes in the layout, using the folded mini-book as a guide. Set the eyelets and thread string through them using the technique shown on page 118. Fix the centre of the mini-book to the background cardstock using photo tabs, then knot the string.

Travellers' fair

I took lots of photographs at the fair, which I wanted to include in the album to give a full flavour of the event but without showcasing all of them. I therefore included them in a mini-book.

Christmas mini-book

This is a variation on the Travellers' fair book. The two sidepieces have been cut into measured points, eyelets set and ribbon threaded through. Green cardstock has been journaled, cut to size and stuck over the sides and base of the book. When tied up (left), the mini-book gives the impression of a parcel – great for Christmas, birthdays or celebrations!

123

Mini-books and page protectors

If you use the type of album where pages slip in to page protectors (called top-loading), then opening the mini-book to look at it can be a problem. There are two solutions. One is to slip the whole page, including the mini-book, into the page protector. The viewer then needs to extract the whole page to look at the mini-book. The alternative, and the example shown here, is to make a hole in the page protector to attach the book or clasp, sticking the mini-book on the outside of the page protector. That way, the rest of the page remains protected.

The Louvre

The mini-book has been made
from pieces of cardstock, which
have been folded concertina style. Note that the book can be made as large as you wish by sticking facing pieces of cardstock together. The photographs were cut to size and fixed on both sides of the book. The eyelet clasp was fitted last. The ribbon was fixed to the underside of the backing cardstock with sticky tape and then pulled through the page protector as shown below.

1. I marked the place for the hole on top of the page protector with photo-safe wax crayon. I then slid the setting mat between the layout and the page protector, made the hole using the hole punch and hammer, then removed the mat.

2. The ribbon was attached to the back of the layout and threaded through the eyelet hole. I then placed the layout in the page protector and fastened the mini-book to the outside of the page protector with photo tabs. Next I put one hand inside the page protector to guide the ribbon through the hole before fastening it to the clasp on the outside of the mini-book in the usual way.

Paris

This mini-book (based on an idea by Joy Aitman) was made using one piece of 30.5 x 30.5cm (12x12in) cardstock, cut into two pieces, one measuring 16.5cm (6½in) and the other 14cm (5½in). The larger piece was folded in half before sticking the smaller piece to it horizontally. I then stuck the photographs into the book, adding embellishments. The technique shown opposite was used to stick the mini-book to the outside of the page protector.

Home

Pages have been cut to accommodate the photograph on the front cover of the mini-book, i.e. 16.5 x 11.5cm (6½ x 4½in). The mini-book was assembled using a collage style. Eyelets were set on the front cover of the book only, and holes were made in identical places on remaining pages. String was threaded through the holes and eyelets and tied to assemble the finished mini-book.

A visit to Toddington

This mini-book has been made very simply by attaching pieces of cardstock together with eyelet snaps. The photographs and text have been sanded and inked to give an aged effect, before being made into a collage in the mini-book.

Tags

Tags are useful for adding accents or dimension to a scrapbook page. Tags can be purchased ready made or you can make your own in any style, colour and design that you wish! Eyelets and tags were meant for each other. Eyelets can be used to fix the tags to the page, provide a means of threading or hanging or just to add that finishing touch.

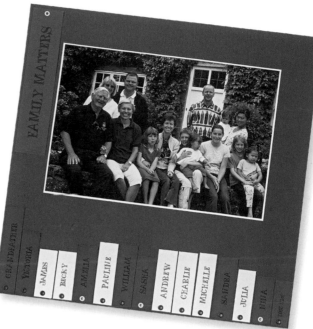

Family matters

Here I have printed the family names as labels. The tags form simple titles.

Brothers

This page is a personal favourite. It shows an old photograph of my father and his eldest brother, now sadly dead. They were very close. I bought these tags, fixed on the letter stickers and stuck the tags to the page as a title, using rub-on paints to coordinate colour with the page.

Seasons

If you are using tags for a title, you do not have to restrict yourself to one letter per tag. Here the tags, made from paper depicting the different months of the year, form a background to the titles of the four seasons.

Tag books

Eyelets can be bought with longer stems which are useful for chunkier items or for making tag books. In these examples, the eyelets in the 'Wild thing' frame and in the 'Winter' tag book are longer than normal, and the eyelet fixing the 'Farm' tag is extra-long. A stock of different sizes proves invaluable. Eyelet tags, like mini-books, make attractive presents as well as items for scrapbook pages.

Seville

Eyelet hinges have been used as part of this tag.

Wild thing

I made a cardstock frame to fit the focal point of the photograph and covered it using the technique shown on page 114.

The vegetable patch

I made a pocket using a seed packet, which I distressed by crumpling it and then using sandpaper and ink. The tags were slipped in the pocket.

Farm

This is one of my favourites, using lots of photographs and rustic embellishments. A long-stemmed eyelet was used to fix the book together and additional eyelets were used with the word 'spring' on one of the tags.

Winter

I made three tags the same size. I put journaling on one, stamped and embossed a tree on another and fixed a photograph on the third, making a little tag book.

Eyelets as accents

Eyelets in all their various guises can be used to make accents with other embellishments, or as tiny accents in their own right. This is where they are at their most versatile and the only limit is your imagination!

Tiny 1mm (¹/₁₆in) eyelets have been used as car wheels.

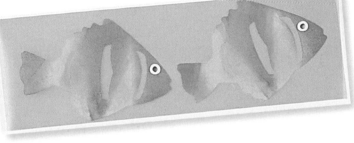

3mm (¹/₈in) white eyelets make eyes for these stamped fish and also fix the vellum to the card.

1mm (¹/₁₆in) eyelets make part of the horse's bridle on this stamped motif.

Red eyelets form the berries for the stamped holly leaves.

White eyelets are used to fix the acetate to this summer scene made from cardstock, paper, a stamped umbrella and a punched sun.

This Christmas slide mount has been decorated with seasonal eyelets.

The May acetate is complemented with flower-shaped eyelets to match the photograph beneath.

This banner has been accented with little musical note-shaped eyelets.

Lilo

This is one of my favourite layouts. Total relaxation! I have applied acrylic paint to the background cardstock with a textured roller. The seahorse, which helps to highlight the theme of the page, is made from white and turquoise acrylic paint mixed together and stamped on with a stamp from a hardware store. Eyelets have been used to make the seahorse's eye and spine.

Trimming the tree

This is an annual tradition in our family. The girls now have it off to a fine art! The tree accents have been made using paper, cardstock and parts of photographs. The eyelets echo the decorations on the tree. They have also been used to trap the tinsel behind the title printed on vellum, which again emphasises the subject matter of the layout.

Aspects of Me

I have chosen this project for three reasons. First, many scrapbookers forget to put themselves in their albums at all. This is to encourage you to do so! Future generations will want to know about you as well as the rest of your friends and family, otherwise there will be an important part of the jigsaw missing.

Secondly, it is one of the only decent photographs I have ever seen of me! Most of the time I am the other side of the lens. I had the photograph taken professionally and strongly recommend that you treat yourself. It really wasn't that scary!

Thirdly, the page can be adapted to any other person you want to showcase in your album, or even a group shot. Eyelets, papers and embellishments were used to complement the words on the 'crossword'. You need to choose styles to complement your own descriptions. My photograph was 14.2 x 18.8cm (5⅝ x 7⅜in). If you have a standard 12.7 x 17.8cm (5 x 7in) sized photograph, you could mat it to fit these dimensions.

You will need

Turquoise cardstock, 30.5 x 30.5cm (12 x 12in)

A photograph of you

Photo tabs

Printed papers to suit your descriptions: I have used check floor, music, greetings, word definition, clocks and handwritten style papers

Scrap paper and pen

Metal letters with eyelet holes

Letter stickers: I have used black stencil, red, silver, circle-framed, variable font and numbered

Ribbons: I have used gingham and lace

Eyelets: I have used plain red, musical note, word, yellow and red heart

Craft knife and cutting mat

Eyelet tool kit

Brads: I have used a flower and a star

Embellishments: I have used a metal heart and a strip of old film negative

Ruler

1. Stick the photograph on the cardstock using photo tabs.

2. To make a tag, take a rectangle of printed paper. Measure and mark 2.5cm (1in) down from the top, and mark this point on the sides. Mark the midpoint of the top edge. Draw a line from the midpoint to the mark on the side, and cut off the corner. Repeat the other side to make the tag shape.

3. Cut rectangles and make tag shapes from all the various types of paper and attach them as shown using photo tabs. Your tags should fit the spaces left by your photograph. My rectangles were, top: 14.5 x 7.2cm (5¾ x 2⅞in); middle left: 11.5 x 5.8cm (4½ x 2¼in); middle right: 11.5 x 7.5cm (4½ x 3in); bottom row all 9.6 x 4.8cm (3¾ x 1⅞in).

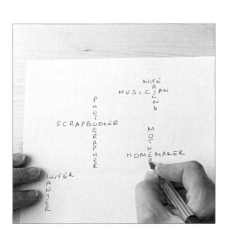

4. I chose nine words to describe me as there are nine tags. Practise writing your chosen words crossword style as shown. When arranging them on the page, I made sure that each tag had part of a word on it.

5. I have used metal letters to spell out the word 'wife'. To fix metal letters, first place them on the layout in the desired arrangement. Then mark where the eyelet will go by using a paper piercing tool. Next attach each letter individually with eyelets.

The finished project. Add the remaining lettering using your handwritten design as a guide. Apart from the word 'wife', I have used stickers for all the lettering. I have chosen black, red and sand-coloured stickers in various different designs. Next, I have fixed eyelets, brads or ribbon to the point of each tag, complementing the words with the style of eyelet where possible. Finally I have added a couple of other embellishments such as the old film negative stuck on with glue and the metal heart.

31ST OCTOBER 2004

POSITIVELY DEFRIGHTFUL!

The children had planning their costumes for weeks! They went out trick-or-treating. — Apparently this custom originated with beggars wandering from village to village and promising to say prayers on behalf of the dead relatives of donors of the "treat" (NICE!!) In those days, the "treat" was currant bread, not sweets. In reality the customs of Halloween grew out of the rituals of the Celts celebrating a new year and out of the medieval prayer rituals of Europeans.

Halloween

The Halloween-style eyelets are both functional and decorative. They have been used to attach the vellum to the cardstock but also as accents in themselves. I have cut round the figures in the photographs to accentuate the subject and dispose of distracting backgrounds. The titles were printed on vellum with embossing powder added to part of the writing just after printing, before the ink dried. The embossing powder was then heated to a raised shine using a heating tool.

Spring in Marlow

Flower eyelets have been used as part of the letters and to affix the journaling, helping to emphasise the spring theme.

Wet

I have used eyelets as part of the letters to accentuate the title and the impression of water.

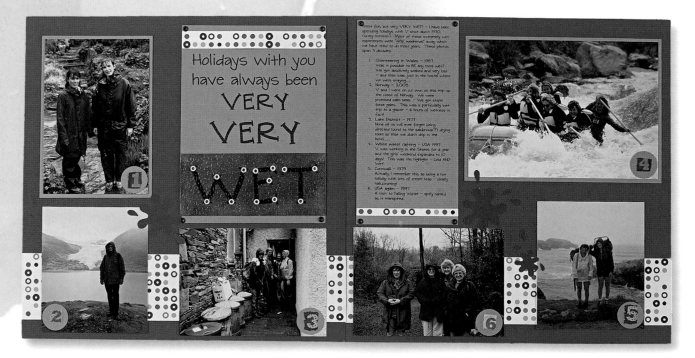

Skiing

I have used lots of different snow- and holiday-related eyelets as accents, including various eyelet words, so that a collage effect is created from eyelets and other embellishments. The edge of the background cardstock was embossed using part of a snowflake stamp and white embossing powder, heated with a heating tool.

Messing About on the River

The idea with this project is to cut photographs and card in wavy lines to emphasise the water theme. The eyelets are placed to add a sense of movement and to give an impression of water droplets. This project could be adapted to any water-based photographs such as seaside, lakes, swimming pool, water sports or even a child playing with a sprinkler in the garden!

You will need

Two pieces of dark blue cardstock, 30.5 x 30.5cm (12 x 12in)

Three pieces of pale blue cardstock in the same size

Cream cardstock in the same size

Wavy ruler

Pencil and eraser

Photo tabs

Photographs

Photo-safe wax crayon

Circle cutter and cutting mat

Twelve plain white eyelets

Eyelet tool kit

Brown ship's wheel card embellishment and glue pen

'We Are Family' button embellishment and glue dot

Scissors

1. Use the wavy ruler to draw a line on the blue cardstock.

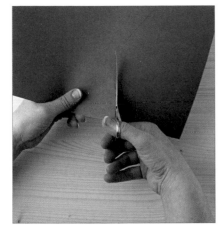

2. Cut out the shape and mount it on the pale blue cardstock using photo tabs.

3. Draw on the photograph using photo-safe wax crayon and a wavy ruler to match the dark blue wavy line on the cardstock.

4. Stick the photograph on to a second piece of pale blue cardstock using photo tabs.

5. Draw three wavy bands on the cream card.

6. Mount the cream wavy line on the left-hand scrapbook page. Use a circle cutter to cut out the chosen part of one photograph.

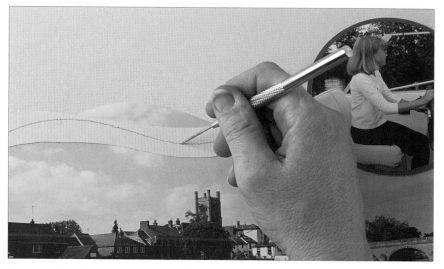

Tip
The wavy line does not need to follow the wave of the cardstock strip exactly. If they are slightly different, this adds to the impression of movement.

7. Use the circle cutter to make a dark blue mat for this photograph. Mount one wavy cream band on the left-hand page, with the matted circular photograph on top. Draw a wavy pencil line on the cream band using the wavy ruler and pierce holes where the eyelets will be fixed. Rub out the pencil line.

The finished project. I printed my title and journaling on pale blue cardstock before mounting them on the dark blue cardstock. All photographs and mats were adhered using photo tabs. I used a glue dot for the button as these are very good for heavier embellishments and a glue pen for the ship's wheel as the pen provided a neat, thin line of glue.

8. Set eyelets where pierced holes have been made. Assemble the wavy bands, photographs and journaling for both pages as shown. Then add the final embellishments.

Tip

Ensure that you rub out the pencil lines before setting the eyelets but after piercing. It is difficult to rub out pencil lines once the eyelets have been set.

Pass the parcel

The idea with all the layouts on these two pages and the 'Messing About on the River' project, is to use eyelets for emphasis. Here, I have used a dinner plate to draw the circle where the eyelets appear. Otherwise I have used the same techniques for arranging and setting the eyelets as in the project. I like the way the circle of eyelets and parcel stickers help to emphasise the subject of the layout.

Easter egg hunt

I have cut out little oval egg shapes, stamped them with gold ink and set eyelets in each of them before adding stickers to make the title. They have then been strung onto fibre. The title complements the photographs.

In the meadow we can build a snowman

I have made the snowman by cutting out circles and covering them in textured paste. The various different eyelets have been used to complete the accent, which derives from the photographs.

Swing

Everything on this layout has been placed at an angle to draw out the swinging motion. The string has been attached through eyelets to elongate the swing and to show that this is what the page is all about. Even the way that the sand-coloured cardstock is cut adds to the feeling of movement.

Index